CALLING MORE SAINTS

CALLING MORE SAINTS

BROTHER TOM-NICHOLAS, FOCD

Troitsa Books
Commack, New York

Editorial Production:	Susan Boriotti
Office Manager:	Annette Hellinger
Graphics:	Frank Grucci and Jennifer Lucas
Information Editor:	Tatiana Shohov
Book Production:	Donna Dennis, Patrick Davin, Christine Mathosian and Tammy Sauter
Circulation:	Maryanne Schmidt
Marketing/Sales:	Cathy DeGregory

Library of Congress Cataloging-in-Publication Data
Tom-Nicholas, Brother.
    Calling more saints / by Brother Tom-Nicholas.
       p.   cm.
    ISBN 1-56072-728-4
    1. Christian saints--Biography. 2. Christian saints--Meditations. I. Title.
BX4657.T643   1999   99-052423
270'.092'2--dc21   CIP
[B]

Copyright © 2000 by Brother Tom Nicholas, FOCD
    Troitsa Books, a division of
    Nova Science Publishers, Inc.
    227 Main Street, Suite 100
    Huntington, New York 11743
    Tele. 516-424-6682   Fax 516-424-4666
    e-mail: Novascience@earthlink.net
    e-mail: Novascil@aol.com
    Web Site: http://www.nexusworld.com/nova

All rights reserved. No part of this book may be reproduced, stored in a retrieval system or transmitted in any form or by any means: electronic, electrostatic, magnetic, tape, mechanical photocopying, recording or otherwise without permission from the publishers.

The authors and publisher have taken care in preparation of this book, but make no expressed or implied warranty of any kind and assume no responsibility for any errors or omissions. No liability is assumed for incidental or consequential damages in connection with or arising out of information contained in this book.

This publication is designed to provide accurate and authoritative information with regard to the subject matter covered herein. It is sold with the clear understanding that the publisher is not engaged in rendering legal or any other professional services. If legal or any other expert assistance is required, the services of a competent person should be sought. FROM A DECLARATION OF PARTICIPANTS JOINTLY ADOPTED BY A COMMITTEE OF THE AMERICAN BAR ASSOCIATION AND A COMMITTEE OF PUBLISHERS.

Printed in the United States of America

DEDICATION

To my wife, Susan, who still loves me after all these years;

To Reverend Mary Gray-Reeves, who encouraged me to try out most of these stories as weekly sermons at St. James;

And to Debra Matsumoto, my personal editor and English teacher:

You go, Girls!

Contents

DEDICATION	v
INTRODUCTION	ix
ELIZABETH SETON – JANUARY 4	1
AGNES – JANUARY 21	5
LYDIA AND PHOEBE – JANUARY 29	7
ABSALOM JONES – FEBRUARY 13	11
POLYCARP – FEBRUARY 23	15
CUTHBERT – MARCH 20	17
MARK THE EVANGELIST – APRIL 25	21
DAME JULIAN OF NORWICH – MAY 8	23
BRENDAN THE NAVIGATOR– MAY 16	27
FLORENCE NIGHTINGALE – MAY 18	29
BERNARDINO OF SIENA - MAY 20	33
BERNARD OF MONTJOUX – MAY 28	35
COLUMBA – JUNE 9	37
EPHREM OF EDESSA – JUNE 10	39
JOHN THE BAPTIST – JUNE 24	41
BRIDGET OF SWEDEN – JULY 23	43
JOSEPH OF ARIMATHEA – JULY 31	45
FRANZ JAGERSTATTER – AUGUST 9	49
MARY THE VIRGIN MOTHER OF CHRIST – AUGUST 15	53
HELENA – AUGUST 19	57

AUGUSTINE OF HIPPO – AUGUST 28	59
DAVID OAKERHATER – SEPTEMBER 1	63
MOTHER TERESA OF CALCUTTA – SEPTEMBER 5	65
JOHN HENRY HOBART – SEPTEMBER 12	69
SERGIUS OF RUSSIA – SEPTEMBER 25	71
TERESA OF AVILA – OCTOBER 15	75
MARTIN OF TOURS - NOVEMBER 11	79
HUGH OF LINCOLN – NOVEMBER 17	81
HILDA OF WHITBY – NOVEMBER 18	85
FRANCIS XAVIER – DECEMBER 3	89
EUSEBIUS OF VERCELLI – DECEMBER 16	93
THOMAS BECKET – DECEMBER 29	97

INTRODUCTION

In the Early Church, the title "saint" was used by St. Paul and his successors to apply to the whole Christian community, "those who keep the faith." Then the term was applied specifically to martyrs during the persecutions, and later, to outstanding local personalities by public acclamation. By the 10th Century, it was decided that the pope had to have the final say on who would be officially considered a saint in the church calendar. However, it wasn't until 1634 that the Roman Catholic Church set up the formal process of nomination, research, hearings, beatification status, formal investigation of three miracles, and final canonization of the saint. The process now takes many years from nomination to decree of sainthood.

In the American Episcopal Church, the official list of saints is contained in the book *Lesser Feasts and Fasts,* an approved set of Collects (opening prayers), Epistles, and Gospel readings for each saint's special commemoration day. These readings are used in the weekly liturgy to honor those men and women that have lived exemplary lives of faith. No miracles are required. New additions to the official list are submitted to a committee, who send their recommendations to be voted on by delegates, both lay and ordained, at the next General Convention of the Episcopal Church, which is held every three years (for example, Florence Nightingale was elected into the Episcopal Calendar at last year's General Convention). We actually share many of the same saints as in the Roman calendar. When the Protestant Reformation kicked in, the saint list was pretty much frozen on the Anglican side of the fence until interest in saints was renewed in the late 19th Century.

But no matter the particular list or special requirements, it's not canonization that makes a man or woman a saint. It is the content of their virtuous lives, whether they are officially recognized by the world or not. Saints are the heroes and heroines of our Christian life, role models we can all look up to for guidance and inspiration regardless of time, place, social standing, or religious denomination.

May these little stories give you the hope, the courage, and the inspiration to try to become the hero or heroine that God knows you can be.

Br. Tom

ELIZABETH SETON – JANUARY 4

Elizabeth was born in New York City on August 28, 1774. Her relatives included some of the most powerful and influential families in Colonial America (in fact, Teddy Roosevelt and Franklin Delano Roosevelt are distant relations). Her mother was the daughter of the Episcopalian Rector of St. Andrew's Church, and Elizabeth's father was a noted physician and anatomy professor at King's College (which later became Columbia University). It was her father who undertook Elizabeth's education, for her mother died when she was only three years old.

In 1794 Elizabeth married a wealthy young merchant, William Magee Seton, and they had two sons and three daughters. Elizabeth devoted much of her time to charity work, and founded The Society for the Relief of Poor Widows. So active was her group in serving the poor that Elizabeth became known at the time as "the Protestant Sister of Charity."

But then the Seton family's shipping business went bankrupt. William's father died, and William himself became ill with tuberculosis. Elizabeth, her two oldest children, and William sailed to Italy in hopes the sunny climate would bring about a cure, but it was not to be. He died there in December 1803. Elizabeth remained in Italy, staying with friends, until the May of the following year, and during that time became very interested in the Roman Catholic Church.

When she returned to America and was re-united with all of her children, Elizabeth faced major opposition from her family and friends regarding the idea of her becoming a Catholic. The major argument was the question of her family's good name and social standing in the community. The Roman Church in New York was predominantly the church of new immigrants, mostly poor Irish. It was felt that Elizabeth would be throwing away her education, her social standing, and her children's chances for a better life just to worship and associate with the unwashed, lower classes of New York. But Elizabeth persevered and became a Roman Catholic in 1805. This decision cut her off from her family and left her with severe financial problems. She was now a single mother, the sole support of five young children. Her relatives and society friends refused to even loan her money to pay her household bills.

So Elizabeth went to work. She gave private French lessons. She ran a boarding house for 14 boys from a nearby school. Her older children had to get jobs to help out. They no longer had happy, carefree lives. Elizabeth became so depressed she considered moving the family to Canada, hoping life would be easier for them there.

But then an invitation came from a Roman Catholic priest to establish a school for girls in Baltimore. Elizabeth and the children moved and the school opened in June 1808. Once settled in Baltimore with a small but steady income, Elizabeth remembered her old Society for Widows, and decided to form another group, only this time the members would all be nuns. She gathered a group of like-minded women, and in the Spring of 1809 formed a community, the Sisters of St. Joseph. From that time onwards Elizabeth, as their superior, was known as Mother Seton.

In June of that same year, Mother Seton and her community established headquarters in the town of Emmitsburg in northwestern Maryland and there, with some modifications and adaptations, her sisters followed the rule of the Daughters of Charity of St. Vincent de Paul. By 1812 twenty women, including her oldest daughter and her two sisters-in-law, had joined the order, now officially known as the Daughters of Charity of St. Joseph.

In 1814 the sisters opened St. Joseph's Orphanage in Philadelphia, and another one in New York City three years later. Wherever her nuns opened a convent, they also started a grammar school. For this reason Mother Elizabeth Seton is often considered the founder of the parochial school system in the United States.

While acting as Mother Superior to her growing congregation, Elizabeth continued to work with the poor and the sick, and still found time to compose music, write textbooks, translate books from French to English, train teachers, and write articles on spiritual life.

Then the time came when she herself was diagnosed with tuberculosis. Elizabeth died at her order's headquarters in Emmitsburg on January 4, 1821. She was only 47 years old. At the time of her death, her congregation of nuns, the first to be founded in America, numbered some twenty communities spread across the United States.

What is most striking about the life of Elizabeth Seton is her heroism in the face of so much sorrow and loss. She outlived most of the members of her family. Her mother died when she was three; her father died of yellow fever; her husband died when she was only twenty-nine; her two sisters-in-law who had joined her Order both died young; and two of her daughters also died of tuberculosis ("our family's disease," as Elizabeth called it in letters to friends).

The eventual deaths of those we love is an undeniable part of our lives here on earth. Mother Seton confronted the same challenges and losses we all must face as children, parents, and friends. She realized that we can either grow from our sufferings or else allow the pain and despair to destroy us. St. Elizabeth chose to look beyond the suffering and develop a deeper sense of love and compassion. Instead of crying, "Why me, Lord?" she used her time and energy to reach out to the other lonely ones in need. St. Elizabeth had every reason to wallow in self-pity for all the tragedies in her life, but instead she remains a shining example of someone who did not so much seek to be consoled as to console, and who did not seek to be loved as much as to share her love with others.

AGNES – JANUARY 21

Agnes was a martyr who died in Rome around 304 during the persecution under Emperor Diocletian. After she refused to offer incense to the Roman gods, the executioners tried to burn her at the stake, but when she remained untouched by the flames, she was beheaded. She is said to have been only 12 or 13 when she died.

Her execution shocked many of the non-Christian Romans and raised questions that helped turn the tide of public opinion toward the Christians. Questions such as: is it not against Roman law to put a virgin to death? Are young girls such a threat to Rome that they must be executed? And what is it about this new religion that enables 12-year-old girls to face death rather than just go through the motions of offering tribute to the old gods?

Either Emperor Constantine's mother, St. Helena, or his daughter, Constantina, built a magnificent basilica at Agnes' tomb in Rome in honor of the young martyr. This early basilica was replaced in the 7th century by St. Agnes' Church, which still stands in Rome.

The earliest depiction of her (as a young girl with hands outstretched in prayer) was carved in a marble plaque in that first basilica. She is usually shown in paintings as holding a lamb (referring to her name in Latin), sometimes also holding either a palm or sword, referring to her martyrdom. There is a carved 18th century Mexican statue of her at Mission Santa Ines Virgen y Martir in Solvang, California, the 19th of the early California missions, which was founded in her name in 1804. And here's some saintly trivia: in medieval times they believed that a girl who went to bed without supper on the eve of St. Agnes' Day would dream that night about her husband-to-be.

The moral of this story is realizing that Agnes was the age of junior high students today. They face a whole new world of problems and fears that we never had to face. They need help and guidance and Christian role models from adults who care: parents, teachers, coaches, and church leaders. We honor the life of young St. Agnes by deciding to make a difference in the lives of our young people, who truly are our future. Why not reach out and change a young person's life for the better today?

LYDIA AND PHOEBE – JANUARY 29

Lydia was born in Thyatira in western Turkey. She later settled in Philippi in Macedonia, north of Greece, a major crossroads for commerce between Asia and Rome. She was a purple dye merchant, which meant she was quite a wealthy businesswoman. The dye was extracted by a difficult process from a certain type of shellfish, so only the upper classes could afford to have clothing dyed that color. In Philippi she was able to market this expensive purple-dyed cloth among the social elite, military retirees, and ruling families. The Bible doesn't mention if she was married or not, but it's possible she may have been a widow who devoted herself completely to her business.

Lydia seems to have been the leader of a small prayer group of women who would meet regularly. Paul and Silas came to town one day and visited the group. Lydia, though a Gentile, knew of the one God of the Jews and was touched by Paul's message of Christ. After hearing him speak, she became Europe's first Christian convert, and her entire household was converted as well. She invited Paul and Silas to stay in her house for some time, teaching the new converts of Philippi. Luke and Timothy also appear to have been visitors to Lydia's place.

She opened her doors again to Paul and Silas when they escaped from prison. Her home became the first European "home church," and Lydia was recognized as a great spiritual leader who helped Paul and his companions spread the Gospel. She was also a successful

Christian woman in the marketplace, since she remained one of the most successful and influential woman in town. There's no indication that Lydia gave up her business after becoming a Christian, but lots of evidence that she used her wealth wisely and generously in the service of the early Church.

Phoebe was another women minister in the early Church. St. Paul introduces her in his Epistle to the Romans, and she was most likely the actual messenger who delivered that letter to the Christian group in that city. Phoebe was deaconess of the church at Cenchrea, a seaport on the eastern side of the city of Corinth. Corinth was on a narrow isthmus that connected southern Greece with northern Greece and the European mainland. She must have been a woman of some wealth and position or she could not have traveled as she did from Cenchrea, a port district of Corinth, all the way to Italy as St. Paul's courier.

Paul's letter also contained his appeal to the Roman Christians to receive Phoebe with all due respect and to aid her in her ministry in any way. In Romans 16:1-2, Paul describes her as "our sister Phoebe, a deaconess of the church...I ask you to receive her in the Lord in a way worthy of the saints and to give her any help she may need...for she has been a great help to many, including me." She was well known as a patron of the unprotected and despised, someone who came to the aid of converts in need. There is an indication that Paul himself might have been ill on one of his visits to Corinth and that she nursed him through his sickness. No doubt her home was a meeting place for the Christians in the area, just as St. Lydia's was in Philippi.

Lydia and Phoebe both were women of influence and ability and both served in leadership positions under St. Paul. He has the reputation of being something of a male chauvinist pig with regard to women. He's often attributed the idea that women should sit down, keep quiet, and never attempt to teach or lead the men. But the stories of Lydia and Phoebe would seem to prove that theory false. Even a hard-nosed apostle like Paul praised these two women, and held them up to all as examples of outstanding Christian leadership. Proving once again that rich or poor, young or old, male or female, God has need of us and our special talents. And He gives us those talents and skills not for personal gain and glory, but so that we, too, like Saints Lydia and Phoebe, can reach out and touch the lives of others with love.

ABSALOM JONES – FEBRUARY 13

Absalom Jones was born in 1746 in Delaware. But what makes his story different from all the other children born in colonial New England was that his parents were both slaves. True, life was better than being a field slave in the plantations down South and his family had some advantage by working as domestic servants, but Absalom could never forget that he was still considered property. This was brought home to him in no uncertain terms when he was 16 years old. He was suddenly separated from his family and sold to a store owner in Philadelphia. Absalom came to believe that knowledge was power, that ignorance was bondage, and that education and learning were his way out of slavery.

His owner was impressed by his abilities and encouraged Absalom to attend a night school for blacks that was operated by the Quakers. Absalom met his future wife at this school, and two years later they were married. He saved enough money to buy his wife's freedom, and then worked and saved for many years more to buy his own. On their 18th wedding anniversary, he was finally a free man. He was 38 years old.

Absalom and his wife became active members of St. George's Methodist Episcopal Church in Philadelphia, where Absalom served as a lay minister and Sunday School teacher for the black members of the congregation. Absalom and his good friend, Richard Allen, another black Sunday school teacher, were so good at making people feel welcome and appreciated during worship and bible study that the black membership at St. George's increased rapidly. Unfortunately, this alarmed the white vestry members, and in 1786 they took a vote and decided that the Black members should be segregated. From now on they could only sit in the balcony area for all church services. On the following Sunday, ushers tapped the two Sunday school teachers on the shoulder during the opening prayers and demanded that they immediately move to the balcony. Absalom and Richard stood up and then walked out of the church, followed by all the other black members.

In 1787 the former parishioners joined with other black Christians to organize the Free African Society. Members paid dues to help others in need, and Absalom and Richard, who had been elected as officers, taught classes and led prayer services. In 1792 the Society collected funds to build a church. Absalom wanted to find a way to once again be part of the Episcopal Church, but Richard was against the idea. So in 1793 the two friends split up. Richard formed his own Methodist congregation, and in 1816 started a new denomination, the African Methodist Episcopal (AME) Church.

Absalom began a series of conferences with William White, the Episcopal Bishop of Philadelphia, who was also one of the first Presiding Bishops of the Episcopal Church. Bishop White agreed to accept the new group as an Episcopal parish, and licensed Absalom as lay reader. It was agreed that after a period of study and if he was found qualified, Absalom would be ordained and serve as rector of the new church. In October 1794, the church built by the Free African Society was dedicated as the St. Thomas African Episcopal Church. Absalom Jones, who was ordained a deacon by Bishop White in 1795 and a priest in 1802, was the first black American to receive formal ordination as a clergyman in any denomination.

St. Thomas Church soon grew to over 500 members in a few years, largely due to the inspired preaching and ministry of Absalom. He was kind and soft-spoken to all who were troubled or in need, and made it a point to visit each family in his parish several times during the year. He also became an outspoken abolitionist leader during the early 1800s, and debated those who claimed that slavery was accepted in the Bible. Rev. Absalom reminded them that "God was the Father who always acted on behalf of the opposed and distressed," and that they must "clean their hands of slavery."

St. Absalom could have easily have taken the road of turning his back on the Church due to his experience of prejudice. Instead, "The Black Bishop of the Episcopal Church" dedicated his life to serving it and its people, and doing whatever he could to change it for the better. His persistent faith in God and his loving desire to make things better are a powerful example for all those who feel trapped by fate or their lot in life. Like St. Absalom, having faith in God and faith in yourself will give you the power to make a difference.

POLYCARP – FEBRUARY 23

St. Polycarp was the Bishop of Smyrna (now known as Izmir) on the west coast of Turkey. He was part of a group of early bishops called "The Apostolic Fathers" who received instruction directly from the Apostles. In Polycarp's case, he was a disciple of St. John the Evangelist. He was also a close friend of St. Ignatius of Antioch and a teacher to St. Irenaeus, two other famous theologians of the early Church, and both of them mention Polycarp in their writings. Polycarp was greatly loved and respected by all the Christians in the Eastern Church.

He was chosen to journey to Rome to meet with Pope Anicetus to discuss disputes between the Western and Eastern Churches, such as the correct date to celebrate Easter. Neither could convince the other to change his position, but out of respect to Polycarp, the Pope agreed that East and West could follow their own local customs and still be one in charity and brotherhood.

A persecution broke out in the Eastern Empire during the time of Marcus Aurelius, around 155 A.D. The faithful pleaded with Bishop Polycarp to leave the country and save himself, but he refused. When the Imperial Guard came to arrest him at night, Bishop Polycarp met them at the door, invited them in to supper, and just asked that he have some time for prayer before he went with them to the prison.

Brought before the tribunal, Polycarp was asked by the sympathetic proconsul to simply deny Christ and accept Caesar as a technicality, and then he would be free to go. Polycarp replied, "For

86 years I have served my King and He has done me no wrong. How then can I now deny my King and Savior? If you require me to swear by Caesar, hear my free confession: I am a Christian; and if you desire to learn the doctrines of Christianity, appoint a time and hear me; we are taught to give due honor to all princes, so far as is consistent with our faith."

The proconsul felt truly sorry for the kindly old man, but could not change the official sentence of death. Polycarp was taken away to be burned at the stake, but when the fire was lit, he was stabbed to death with a spear by order of the proconsul so that he would not have to suffer. The government officials, afraid of an uprising, made a formal proclamation to the proconsul advising him not to allow a place of burial for fear the local Christians, "abandoning the Crucified Man, should worship Polycarp instead." But Polycarp's friends were allowed to give his remains an honorable burial. And note that we have "Pontius Pilate/Christ – Proconsul/Polycarp" similarities here, something that was not lost on the Christians at the time.

St. Polycarp was a caring and loving Christian who impressed everyone who knew him or knew of him. Sometimes we seem to be so zealous of making points and winning arguments that the kindness and love that Christ showed to all gets lost by the wayside. St. Polycarp lived and died as a beacon of Christian love to believers and non-believers alike. With all the divisions and strife we see in the world today, maybe it's time to follow his loving example, and seek the grace and strength to go forth and do likewise.

CUTHBERT – MARCH 20

Cuthbert was born in Northumbria in northern England around 625. One night, when he was a teenager and working at his full-time shepherd job, he saw a series of lights in the sky. Cuthbert thought it looked as if a soul were being escorted heavenward by a band of angels. A few days later he learned that St. Aidan of Lindisfarne had died that night, so Cuthbert decided this was a sign that God wanted him to give up the shepherd job and enter the monastic life.

However, it appears he didn't immediately sign up. Legend has it young Cuthbert was drafted into the army to fight against the Mercians. It wasn't until after the war was over that we hear of a spear-carrying Cuthbert arriving on horseback at the gates of Melrose Abbey, asking permission to become a monk. Legend or not, he was accepted, and stayed at the Abbey from 651 to 664.

When the Abbot (St. Eata) was made the bishop of Lindisfarne, Cuthbert was chosen to accompany him and made prior (religious superior) of the new monastery there. Although his real preference was for the solitary life of a hermit, he recognized his duty to minister to the needs of the common people. Year after year he made long journeys, on horseback and on foot, to Durham and throughout Northumbria, preaching to the people in remote areas and instructing them in the faith. When a plague struck that area, Cuthbert became famous for convincing the people to pray to God and put their trust in His mercy and love in times of sickness, rather than relying on charms, amulets, and religious superstitions.

Like St. Francis of Assisi, Cuthbert was well-known for having a remarkable rapport with animals, and many legends are told of his adventures with animals, both wild and domestic. One story tells of how he was staying with a poor widow and her young son during one of his missionary journeys. He and the boy were walking along a river when the little boy mentioned how hungry he was. Cuthbert suggested they both pray for something to eat. As they were praying, a magnificent eagle swooped down from the sky into the water, re-emerging seconds later with a large salmon and dropped it at the boy's feet. The boy was overjoyed at this turn of events and picked up the fish to take home for dinner. Cuthbert tells the boy," Don't you think that we should share this with our kind fisherman?" The boy agrees, so Cuthbert cuts the fish in half and has the boy throw half the salmon back. The eagle swoops down, retrieves his half, and disappears into the sky. And so dinner for four was provided by God: Cuthbert, the boy, his widowed mother, and the faithful eagle.

Another legend tells of Cuthbert and his monks praying all night by the seashore. Just before dawn, Cuthbert walks into the sea up to his knees, singing the day's psalm of praise. Returning to shore he kneels down, still praying, when two sea otters appear on the beach. They scramble up to Cuthbert's cold feet, breathe their warm otter-breath on his feet, and dry them with their thick, warm fur. Good St. Cuthbert blesses them and they scurry back into the sea.

Cuthbert later decided to spend the rest of his life as a hermit, devoting all his time to prayer and meditation. So he built a little 2-room shelter on the island of Farne, not far from Lindisfarne. He loved the small island and his time alone, but he was not without visitors. Some of his monks would be allowed to come from time to time, and the King himself once arrived for a visit to ask Cuthbert to leave the island and become a bishop to help mediate growing problems between Church leaders in Rome and those in Britain. Cuthbert didn't want to accept any high office in the Church, but was finally convinced that this was part of God's plan, and so he reluctantly accepted. Theodore, the Archbishop of Canterbury, made Cuthbert the Bishop of Hexham. But Cuthbert managed to get permission to exchange dioceses with his old friend St. Eata, and Cuthbert was allowed to stay home and became the bishop of Lindisfarne. Two years later, Bishop Cuthbert felt his time on earth was coming to a close, so he retired to his beloved island of Farne with a few of his monks and died there the following year.

An interesting aspect of St. Cuthbert's life was that while he had his religious life all planned out as a solitary hermit on his little island, God had other plans. When St. Cuthbert got the call to serve as bishop, he didn't want the job and tried hard to get out of it. But he knew deep down that he had the God-given talents to serve others as a teacher, leader, and peacemaker, and so he knew he had to answer God's call. There are times in our own lives when we know the right thing to do, but yet we try so hard to avoid helping out, volunteering, or taking the time to give of ourselves. It's so easy to want to stay in our own little world, safe in our private cocoon, only doing what we want and only when we want to do it. But God has other plans for us as well. Think about the example of St. Cuthbert: take the time to reach out to others, so that you, too, can fly with the eagles ... and possibly share unexpected seafood dinners with those you love.

St. Cuthbert

MARK THE EVANGELIST – APRIL 25

Mark was not one of the Twelve Apostles, but from the New Testament we learn that he was related to St. Barnabas and was a Levite (Levites were the only tribe of Israel that were allowed to assist the priests in the ceremonies of the Temple in Jerusalem–sort of an all-male Altar Guild). His mother's house was a meeting place and home church for Christians in Jerusalem. Paul and Barnabas took Mark with them to help out in their missionary journey to Cyprus, but Mark seems to have gotten homesick. He left the group when they reached Pamphylia and returned to Jerusalem. Consequently, St. Paul considered young Mark to be something of a flake, and refused to include him when plans for the next trip to Asia Minor came up. Barnabas disagreed and sided with Mark, which resulted in the break-up of the famous missionary team of Paul and Barnabas. Paul continued with Silas as his assistant, while Barnabas took Mark with him back to Cyprus.

But Mark evidently changed his ways because, when Paul was first imprisoned in Rome, he mentioned that Mark was there to help him. And in Paul's second captivity, shortly before he was martyred, Paul wrote to Timothy at Ephesus and told him to "take Mark and bring him with you, for he is profitable to me for the ministry."

In his role as author of one of the Gospels, St. Mark has been called the interpreter of St. Peter. It seems that when Mark went to Rome to stay with Paul, he also became good friends with Peter who had also moved there. Mark wrote down all the stories he heard Peter tell about the life and teachings of Christ. Tradition says that after the deaths of Saints Peter and Paul, Mark left Rome and moved to Alexandria in Egypt where he eventually became a bishop. Venice, Italy claims to have the tomb of St. Mark, which is supposed to have been brought there from Alexandria in the 7th century, and this is how he got the honor of being the Patron Saint of Venice.

Back in the time of Saints Augustine and Jerome, the "four living creatures" from the Book of Revelation (a man, a lion, an ox, and an eagle) were considered to symbolize the four evangelists (Matthew, Mark, Luke, and John). Jerome and Augustine considered the lion to represent St. Mark because his Gospel opens with John the Baptist crying out in the desert, and lions could be heard roaring in the desert back in those days.

St. Mark teaches us that everyone has the ability to change for the better. No matter what we've done in the past, we can repent, renew, and start over. St. Mark grew up and learned what it was to make a commitment to others and to Christ and not give up when thing don't go our way. St. Paul learned to forgive and forget. They managed to eventually reconcile as true friends and brothers in Christ. So when the people in your world are making you crazy, think about St. Mark: "...forgive us our trespasses, as we forgive those who trespass against us."

DAME JULIAN OF NORWICH – MAY 8

In the Middle Ages, the solitary religious life was quite popular in various forms. There were hermits, solitary men who didn't stay in one place, but would move from one area to another according to circumstances. In England, their service to God and man often entailed taking care of roads and bridges, serving as religious highway repairmen. A anchorite or anchoress, like Dame Julian, was someone who was voluntarily shut away from normal social life, and was enclosed in an anchorage (little house), primarily to spend time in prayer and contemplation.

Almost every town in those days wanted to have at least one religious recluse, and most contributed money to maintain them. Having a wise, holy person living in your hometown was thought to be a way to avoid natural disasters, like plagues and floods. Equally important to the town fathers was the fact that recluses were something of a religious tourist attraction, bringing in pilgrims to visit and spend money in the local inns and shops. The 14th Century has been called the Golden Age of the English Recluse. Besides Dame Julian in Norwich, records show six recluses living in Winchester, two at Lincoln, and at least eight in London, living in dwellings attached to churches, monasteries, convents, and castles.

How did you become an anchorite? First you had to be investigated by an church official appointed by the local bishop, usually an archdeacon, abbot, or abbess. In addition, you had to show that you had the money to support yourself in permanent enclosure.

This meant that most recluses were of the upper classes with trust funds. If you were poor, you had to become a nun, monk, or one of those bridge-building hermits. If you could satisfy these requirements, the bishop would officially list you in the church records as an anchorite, and in a special religious ceremony, enclose you in your anchorage.

An anchorage was not a tiny cell as in some monasteries or convents. Since these were well-to-do lay people who took modified vows and did not live in absolute poverty, the typical English anchorage was simple but comfortable: a suite of several rooms or a bungalow surrounded by its own fenced garden. And very few recluses lived in absolute solitude. Most had servants to handle their business affairs and do the shopping, cooking, and cleaning. It was a life of self-denial and prayer, but not one cut off from human contact. Visitors were allowed. You could visit Dame Julian in her little bungalow next to the parish church in Norwich, but she was bound by her rule as an anchoress to never leave the premises until she died.

Dame Julian was born in 1342 in Norwich, England of a noble family. When she was 30 years old and still living in her mother's house, Julian was struck down by an illness so serious that everyone thought she was dying. On May 8, 1373, the third Sunday after Easter, a priest was summoned to give her the last rites. Before he left, the priest gave her a crucifix, and placed it where she could see it from her bed. He suggested Dame Julian meditate on the face of the crucified Christ to give her comfort in her last days on earth. As Dame Julian began to pray and meditate, she experienced a series of sixteen revelations, or "showings" as she called them, throughout the night. When she awoke the next morning, she had miraculously recovered from her illness.

Some time later, she decided to dedicate her life to God, not as a nun in a convent, but as an solitary anchoress. Dame Julian became well known as a Christian mystic, and many people came to her little bungalow in Norwich to seek her advice and direction in their spiritual lives. By all accounts she was a very kind and learned woman, not just some ethereal virgin-saint with her head in the clouds, but a wise and practical spiritual director. She decided to write down her spiritual revelations from that night in May, and the result became a famous book, *The Revelation Of Divine Love.*

Her book begins as a simple Good Friday meditation on the passion and death of Christ, then moves to a much larger theological discussion of creation, unconditional love, why sin exists, how suffering can be an educational experience to bring us closer to God, and how God's loving care is a constant force in the world. She demonstrates a profound understanding of theological thought, far beyond her male medieval contemporaries. For instance, she describes the Father, Son, and Holy Spirit as All-Might, All-Wisdom, and All-Love in one revelation, and in another as Life, Love, and Light. She made certain her readers got the message that God is love, and that all His works, both in this world and the next, are done in love. "The lord is God the Father, the servant is the Son, Jesus Christ, and the Holy Spirit is the love that is common to them both."

Dame Julian also introduced a totally unique theological concept: describing Christ in terms of a Divine Mother.

"A kind, loving mother who understands and knows the needs of her child. As the child grows older, she allows the child to be punished so that its faults are corrected and its virtues developed. This way of doing things is Our Lord, as a Mother, at work in us."

It took a woman's touch to challenge the concept of the world as a sinful, unhappy place of constant toil and sickness, ruled by a angry God of retribution and punishment. Dame Julian believed in a world of love and beauty, watched over by a Divine Father who deeply cared about each one of His beloved children. Too often we seem to be programmed to think of God in terms of crime and punishment. St. Julian reminds us that there is a world in our own hearts where we can always find contentment and love. As she herself put it, as long as we have faith, "all will be well, and all will be well, and all manner of things will be well."

St. Julian of Norwich

BRENDAN THE NAVIGATOR– MAY 16

Brendan was born near Tralee on the west coast of Ireland. He was immediately sent to St. Ita's School for Boys for 5 years. When he grew up he became a priest and then decided to become a monk. Brendan soon gathered followers around him and founded a monastery in Clonfert in 559. Clonfert became a major religious and educational center in Ireland, and before Brendan died at age 85, he had 3,000 monks following his Rule of Life.

St. Brendan once wrote that the greatest influence in his life for doing good was having St. Ita as his elementary school teacher. He kept in touch with her over the years, even after he became a famous abbot. He once asked his old teacher to tell him what she considered to be the three things God most truly loves. St. Ita replied, "...the true faith of a pure heart, the simple religious life, and generosity inspired by Christian charity. And now I will tell you what Our Lord most hates: a scowling face, obstinate wrong-doing, and too much confidence in money."

Every few years, Brendan would take a sabbatical from his abbot duties and take to the high seas. He and a few companions made several voyages in animal-skin-covered boats called "coracles" from Ireland to Scotland, and then to England and Wales as missionaries. But his fame as a navigator comes from a 10th Century epic, the *Navigato*. This "Book of Brendan's Voyages" tell how Brendan and his monks sailed westward across the Atlantic to "a land of promise." Some medieval scholars think the stories indicate the group reached

Greenland and North America, while others feel Brendan's destination might have been the Canary Islands.

One famous story from the *Navigato* could be titled: "St. Brendan and the Tale of the Whale." Brendan and the guys landed on a small island where they celebrated Easter Sunday mass. When the service was over, St. Brendan decided they should properly celebrate the feast day, so the monks lit a fire and started to prepare an Easter brunch. That's when they discovered that the island wasn't an island. The monk-sailors had landed on the back of a sleeping whale. The campfire woke up the whale who began to move. St. Brendan quickly ordered the monks back into their little boat, and, thanks be to God, they all escaped before the whale island disappeared under the waves. Adventures like that easily won Brendan the job as patron saint of sailors and explorers.

Sometimes we get the idea that saints were very serious, holy, and boring people who prayed and studied but never had any fun. Not St. Brendan. He worked hard and played hard. He saw no conflict between his two vocations of teaching and exploring. You might consider him a medieval Jacques Cousteau, always ready for adventure, but then returning to civilization to share what he learned. Brendan always sought to educate and inspire his fellow monks and students to respect and admire the wonders of God's creation in earth and sky and sea.

He could have spent his life quietly sitting with his books in his Irish monastery. Instead he took chances and explored brave new worlds, sharing his love of Christ with new people. And that is his special message to us today. Sometimes we need to take risks, to make a leap of faith and travel down a new path in life. It is so easy in today's world of possessions and consumerism to be too comfortable, too insulated, too isolated from the simple things in life. We can hide in our happy, environmentally-controlled cocoons with all the modern conveniences, and never share our good things with others. That's the time to remember St. Brendan. Sometimes taking the risk of giving of ourselves to others can be the greatest adventure of all.

FLORENCE NIGHTINGALE – MAY 18

She was named after her birthplace, Florence, Italy, in 1820 when her upper-class English parents were traveling abroad. Florence was very studious and religious even as a young girl, and in the spring of 1844 when she was 24, she believed she heard the voice of God calling her to make a vocation of nursing the sick. Her parents were horrified. In England in those days nursing was done mostly by disabled army veterans or destitute women with no other means of support. It was common practice for them to be alcoholics and have no medical training whatsoever. The only nurses with any interest in their jobs were nuns, a profession Florence's parents considered equally horrifying for a young lady in society who could marry into a good family.

But Florence could not be shaken from what she was certain was the will of God. She went to Germany to learn nursing from a Lutheran order of deaconesses who ran a hospital in Kaiserwerth. When she returned to England she used the influence of Sidney Herbert, a member of Parliament and a close family friend of the Nightingales, to get her the appointment of superintendent at a private women's hospital in London. People in society began taking note of her innovative work in hospital sanitation and formal training for nurses. But she didn't become a household name until the Crimean War.

Pitting England and France against Russia, the Crimean War was a series of long and bloody military disasters for the British. Reports from war correspondents soon made it clear that war-profiteers and bureaucrats were damaging the war effort. Charles Dickens was moved to write a newspaper editorial about the insufficient clothing, lack of medical supplies, and medical neglect and stupidity in the field and camp hospitals. It was Sidney Herbert's turn (now the Secretary of War) to ask Florence if she would consider training and leading a group of nurses to the main military hospital in Scutari on the north edge of the Black Sea. Florence was ready for the challenge. With a team of 38 hand-picked nurses (10 Roman Catholic nuns, 14 Anglican nuns, and 14 nurses from her London hospital), she set out to battle horrendous working conditions, cholera, and the prejudice of a male medical staff. By appealing to Queen Victoria herself, she overcame opposition and reformed hospital procedures with spectacular results. Newspaper reporters wrote about her visiting the wards at night, carrying a dim light, to make sure none of the soldiers were in need of help. It wasn't long before "The Lady with the Lamp" became a Victorian media star and national heroine. Queen Victoria remarked at the time, "I wish we had her at the War Office instead of all these fools!" and was so impressed with her work that they became lifelong friends.

When the war was over, Florence capitalized on her new-found celebrity by working to build a permanent school for nursing. With the support of the Queen and thousands of individual donations, the Nightingale Training School for Nurses was established at St. Thomas Hospital in 1871. Nurses trained at the Nightingale School became matrons of hospitals around the world. Clara Barton, the founder of the American Red Cross and a long-time friend, was greatly influenced by Florence to set higher standards for the growing nursing profession in America.

Under the strain of constant work, her own health broke, and Florence became an invalid (although a very active one), and was often bed-ridden for the last 30 years of her life in a small house in London. The Queen offered her private rooms in Buckingham Palace, but Florence kindly refused in order to have access to her hospital work at a moment's notice. She also turned down several marriage proposals and never married, preferring to live alone with her work, a few servants, and her menagerie of tabby cats.

Florence Nightingale felt (like Mother Teresa a century later) that nursing the sick should be considered an honorable, almost religious vocation, a way of serving Christ in the poor, the ill, and the helpless. She wrote devotional books as well as nursing manuals, and believed that mystical prayer was not just for monks and nuns, but should be part of every-day life for all Christians. St. Florence felt that seeking God's will in all things should be the goal in life, seeking to serve others rather than our own selfish desires and ambitions. She once wrote in her diary that God spoke to her and said, "You are here to carry out my program. I am not here to carry out yours." Florence continued: "I must remember that God is not my private secretary." That is just as true for us today. God is not here to carry out our own personal agendas and timetables. We are here to carry out His desires and to share His love and compassion with all our brothers and sisters in this world, in spite of occasional disappointments and difficult circumstances. So follow the advice of a no-nonsense, emergency-room nurse like St. Florence: "Get back on the right path to spiritual health and recovery. STAT!"

BERNARDINO OF SIENA - MAY 20

He was born in Siena, Italy in 1380, the son of the local governor. He was orphaned at age 7 and was brought up by his aunt. At 17 Bernardino joined the Hospital of Santa Maria della Scalla at a time when a plague hit the area. Since both staff and patients were dying at the rate of 1 to 2 dozen per day, Bernardino offered to take charge of the hospital along with several of his friends from school. Bernardino and his friends worked day and night for four months, nursing the sick and dying, cleaning up the wards, and bringing in supplies. After it was all over, the stress and long hours caught up with Bernardino, and he ended up with a fever that kept him bedridden for several months.

During his convalescence, he decided to joined the Franciscan Order and work for God full-time. He was ordained a priest in 1403, and it was soon discovered that he had talent as a motivational speaker. He was in demand as a great preacher and traveled across Italy on foot, often delivering several sermons each day. His style attracted huge crowds: he would make them laugh and make them cry, driving home his message with storytelling, acting and some old-fashioned fire and brimstone, depending on the occasion.

Favorite sermon topics included denouncing gambling and the evils of demon rum. He was well known as a master in the art of debate and persuasion, which is how he got the job as patron saint of advertising and public relations. He was also a big promoter of the use of the emblem I.H.S. (the first three letters of the name "Jesus" in

Greek), as a religious symbol in churches and homes. In Italian cities torn apart by violent rival factions and political parties, Bernardino would heal the deadly feuds by persuading the leaders to substitute his monogram of Jesus for their party symbols on the doors of their homes and public buildings.

In Bologna he gave one of his famous sermons denouncing the evils of gambling. The people were so impressed, they gave up all games of chance and brought their cards and dice to be burnt in a public bonfire. A playing-card manufacturer in town complained to St. Bernardino that his only means of income was being destroyed. The saint suggested he start making paper signs of the I.H.S. emblem instead. Demand for the emblems was so great that the card-maker made more money than before.

He was elected vicar-general of the Franciscan Order and held that position of authority for a few years. But he really hated working at a desk and having to handle all kinds of religious paperwork. Bernardino realized that he could serve God and the people best by going back on the road and preaching full-time. So he asked to step down, and his request was finally approved. St. Bernardino was past 60 by this time and rode a donkey to get around, but he still managed to do a 3-hour sermon every day for the next 18 months. He died in 1444 while traveling from Siena to Naples to do yet another lecture series.

When it came to fighting compulsions and bad habits, St. Bernardino had a simple but effective message: we can't do it alone. We need God's help, and we need to be willing to accept His love to break free from our selfish attitudes. And getting a good whack upside the head from a no-nonsense coach like St. Bernardino will definitely keep you on the right path.

BERNARD OF MONTJOUX – MAY 28

Bernard was born in Italy in 996. He became a priest and was made vicar-general of the Diocese of Aosta, and spent the next 40 years doing missionary work in the Alps. He visited every village and town in the area, building schools and churches. Bernard and some of his friends later decided to become Augustinian Canons-Regular, an order of parish priests and lay-brothers who lived in a community like monks.

In those days many religious pilgrims (mainly French and German travelers on the way to Rome) had to cross the Alps through two passes leading to Aosta. But the journey was a dangerous one: many people lost their way in the snowdrifts and froze to death, while others were attacked by robbers. When Bernard heard of this, he decided his mission from God was to the make the pilgrimage journey a safe one and to provide comfort for all poor and needy travelers. First, he single-handedly managed to shame the robbers into leaving the area. Then Bernard and the rest of monks built two Alpine hospices "for lost travelers of all religions and origins" in the two mountain passes that came to be named in his honor: the Great Bernard and the Little Bernard. This feat of love and engineering gained Bernard the title of "Patron Saint of Mountaineers and Skiers."

Is this where we get the stories about St. Bernard dogs carrying little kegs of brandy to lost hikers in the Alps? Well, the brandy kegs may be more legend than fact, but St. Bernard and his monks are considered to have been the first to breed Alpine Mastiffs (better known these days as St. Bernards) to help them in their hospice duties. The large dogs were trained as faithful guide dogs who, because of their keen sense of smell, would never stray from a mountain path, even if it was covered by deep snow. The dogs were also used as pack animals to carry large loads on journeys. Back home, the dogs were so big and strong that they could pull small wagons and carts for the monks when they were out working in the monastery fields, orchards, barns, and dairies.

St. Bernard cared about the health and safety of travelers who were total strangers to him, but he felt Christ wanted him to try to make a difference. He didn't sit back and say, "Oh, what a shame! People are suffering and dying of cold. But if God wants to save them, He can. It's not my job; it's up to God!"

God's will for us is to get up and make life better whenever and wherever we can. So don't just sit back and say, "The world is so horrible, I can't possibly make a difference," and leave it at that. Remember St. Bernard: go out into that cold, cruel world and bring warmth and hope to those in need of your special, loving care.

And by the way, don't forget to let out that big dog when you get back.

COLUMBA – JUNE 9

St. Columba is the most famous Scottish saint in the calendar, although he was actually born in County Donegal, Ireland in 521. He is also known as St. Colmcille or Colum of the Kil ("kil" means "church" or "monk's cell" in Gaelic). In his early life he was said to be fond of "praying, reading, and fighting." He entered a monastery and was ordained a priest at age 25. Columba then spent the next 15 years traveling around Ireland, preaching and founding other monasteries at Derry, Durrow, and Kells. This was a time of rival factions between monarchs and their supporters in the Church. Columba stepped on some rival missionary clergy's toes and found himself on the outs with the royal family of Ireland. Times being what they were, Columba decided to leave Ireland in 563. He set out in a little wicker boat with 12 companions and arrived at the island of Iona off the west coast of Scotland. Columba and his monks set up a monastery there, and used it as a base for missionary voyages to Scotland. Monks from Iona found another missionary station on another island off the east coast of England known as Lindisfarne, the Holy Island. Lindisfarne later became the training school for Aidan and Cuthbert, the other two famous missionary saints of the Celtic Church.

At that time northern Scotland was inhabited by the Picts. Columba converted their king, which caused all the people to follow the royal example. Southern Scotland was ruled over by the Scots. They were in the process of getting a new king. Columba, who had the divine knack of being at the right place at the right time, personally blessed and crowned the new king, converting all the Scots in the process.

When not engaged in missionary or diplomatic expeditions, Columba lived at his monastery at Iona, which grew into a major center of culture and learning. He was often visited by people from all walks of life for both spiritual and physical help, since he developed quite a reputation for performing miracles and giving sound advice. One of the reasons that Columba was so greatly admired and respected by all, including his enemies, was that he was totally unlike many of the soft, worldly clergy of the time. "He was not a gentle hero," according to Adamnan of Iona, his official biographer. He described Columba as more of a macho, thrill-seeking kind of guy. This was a saint who loved to sail his boat into the fiercest of storms, whose voice was like the bellowing of a bull when he preached, and who was always ready to fight for Christ, with a sword if need be, when the occasion arose.

After Columba's death, his influence continued to dominate the Church in Scotland, Wales, England, and Ireland. For more than a century, Celtic Christianity upheld his traditions in matters of authority and ritual, and the Church of Britain was considered a force in all ways equal to the power of the Roman Church traditions until the Synod of Whitby in 663.

St. Columba was not a quiet servant of God who spent all his time in prayer and meditation. He had his share of faults, and could be stubborn, bull-headed, and arrogant. But he was also loving to the sick and helpless, and always ready to take the time to give both physical and spiritual aid to those in need, no matter their position or station in life. He readily admitted his faults and always gave credit for his successes to the grace and mercy of God.

You don't have to be perfect to follow the message of Christ, and thank God for that or we'd all be in trouble. But if we're willing to love God and love our neighbor, just like St. Columba, we can make all the difference in the world.

EPHREM OF EDESSA – JUNE 10

Ephrem was born around 306 in Nisibis in Mesopotamia. He was baptized at age 18 and started working for Bishop James of Nisibis as a teacher in the bishop's school. Ephrem was considered such a great scholar, he was chosen to accompany the bishop to the Council of Nicaea in 325.

In 363, the Persians were given the city of Nisibis as part of a peace agreement with Emperor Jovian, but as a result, all the Christians had to leave town. Ephrem decided the time was right for him to become a hermit-monk, so he retired to a cave overlooking the city of Edessa. He lived on barley bread and vegetables and spent his time writing theological books and essays on the Old and New Testament.

Then the new bishop of Edessa asked Ephrem for his help. He was asked to leave his hermit lifestyle and help out as a deacon, and the hermit-monk reluctantly agreed. Ephrem became one of the first leaders in the church to recognize the potential of sacred songs as a valuable addition to public worship, so he wrote many hymns for a special women's choir he started in Edessa. Needless to say, letting women sing in church was considered a revolutionary idea at the time, but Ephrem had always been a forward-thinking guy. He is still known in the Eastern Church as "The Harp of Holy Spirit" because of his talent as a composer of sacred music.

In 372 there was a great famine in the area, and as deacon, it was Ephrem's job to take charge of the local relief efforts. Church and civil authorities gave him money and supplies to feed the poor, so he started one of the first food banks. Ephrem also come up with the idea of an ambulance service using special wagons to bring the sick to a central hospice facility.

But Ephrem seemed to have exhausted himself in his efforts to serve the sick and the hungry, and once the famine was over, he retired and moved back to his cave. He spent the last few months of his life finishing his memoirs. St. Ephrem is the only deacon honored with the title, "Doctor of the Church."

The moral of this story is that you can't judge by appearances. St. Ephrem was a short, bald little man who always dressed in an old, patched-up monk's habit except during church services, when he had to wear his deacon's vestments. Now a ragged, desert hermit would be the last person you'd expect to show an interest in promoting women's choral music, but St. Ephrem did just that. He looked beyond the standard conventions of his time to see new ways to share Christ's message with others. So the next time someone volunteers to help you in some project, and they don't seem to fit in with your usual group, don't be so quick to dismiss them just because they're different. You'd be surprised at all the people you overlook everyday with hidden, God-given talents that only need a chance to blossom. Like St. Ephrem, we can all learn to take that chance.

JOHN THE BAPTIST – JUNE 24

John was a cousin to the Holy Family, about six months older than Jesus. But by the time the two became adults, it was John who was the big star. For one thing, John was much higher up on the Jewish social ladder. John's father, Zechariah, was a priest, and his mother, Elizabeth, was also a descendant of Aaron, the brother of Moses, so she was related to the priestly class in her own right. And even though John's personal habits make him sound like some long-haired wild man who dressed like Cro-Magnon Man, this was perfectly acceptable for a Jewish prophet.

He had a great following, including the Pharisees, because he preached repentance and following the Law. He obeyed all the rules: he fasted, prayed, and had nothing to do with Gentiles. John told the people to reform their lives, get baptized in the Jordan River to symbolize their repentance, and show charity to others. His austere life and fame as a preacher gained him the veneration and respect of the Jewish people, and many considered him to be the long-expected Messiah. Even King Herod greatly respected John as a holy man, but he also feared John's power and influence on the people, which led to John's eventual imprisonment and death.

Jesus, on the other hand, was considered a blue-collar carpenter, the son of a blue-collar carpenter, so He had no religious or social standing at all. True, He was related to King David, but David and Solomon and the rest of that gang were a pretty immoral crowd. It would be like someone saying he was proud of being related to Herod, the political king of the Jews in the eyes of Rome. You could get beat up for that in Judea in 30 A.D.

Jesus was also considered something of a radical, a rock-and-roll rabbi, if you will. He was considered by most to be a great teacher, but not of the priestly class, and He sometimes bent the Law by talking to women and Gentiles and going to parties with public sinners and tax collectors. Jesus was hated by the priests and Pharisees, as well as the Zealots. It was His cousin, John, who was accepted and endorsed by the religious right of his day, not Jesus, whose motives and teachings were often suspect.

But in spite of St. John's prestige and leadership abilities, he accepted his place as the forerunner of Christ. Even though he could have gone all the way and been a hugely-successful political and religious leader, he realized his time had come to step down and let his cousin, Jesus, take center stage as the true Messiah. "In order for Him to be greater, I must become less." He told his growing entourage to follow Jesus, and accepted the mission of serving Christ and the people rather than pursue his own motives and ambitions.

That's an important lesson for us today when power, money, and prestige, whether in business, government, or even the church, can be such an attractive temptation, seducing us to put our own needs and desires before everyone else, perhaps even God. John had the strength of character and the humility to see where his God-given talents lay, and knew when to put aside his individual wishes to become a follower of his younger cousin's message of love. St. John the Baptist continues to show us the way as we travel through the wilderness of modern life: in order for Jesus to be greater in our lives, we must become less. For only then will Christ be able to find space in our hearts for His faith and hope and love.

BRIDGET OF SWEDEN – JULY 23

Bridget, also known as Brigitta, is the patron saint of Sweden. She was born in 1303 to wealthy parents. Her father was the governor of Upland, the main province of Sweden. At 14 she married Prince Ulf of Nericia and they lived happily together for 28 years with their eight children, one of whom later became St. Catherine of Sweden. For many years, Bridget worked as the principal lady-in-waiting for Queen Blanche of Sweden.

After Ulf died, she lost favor at court, but she was much loved by the common people. She traveled around the country on her white mule, using her wealth to look after their needs. Like many other great women saints, she was not at all shy of criticizing the occasional wayward pope, emperor, bishop, or prince to return to the straight and narrow path of Christ.

Bridget was also famous for her prophecies and revelations about religious and civil problems of the day, like trying to get the pope to bring peace between England and France. She also had a vision to found a religious order for men and women called "the Order of the Most Holy Savior," also known as the Brigittines. The rules and constitutions for the monks and nuns were said to have been dictated to her by Christ Himself in another vision. What in the Middle Ages were considered miraculous visions and revelations might today be called creative thinking and visualization, two areas where we know St. Bridget excelled. At any rate she provided all the funds to build a double monastery at Vadstena. Sixty nuns lived on one side with 85 monks in a separate building across the way. The men were subject to Abbess Bridget in all organizational and financial issues of the monastery, and the women were subject to the Abbott of the monks in all spiritual matters. All surplus income was given away to the poor at the end of each year, but everyone could have as many books for study as he or she wished. It wasn't long before the monastery became the literary center of 14th century Scandinavia.

In 1371 she made a pilgrimage to Rome and the Holy Land as per one of her visions, and after surviving a shipwreck off Jaffa, she and her companions had a wonderful trip that she later wrote about in one of her books. She returned to Rome where she came down with a fever, and after several months of illness, she died there at the age of 73.

St. Bridget didn't feel that you had to give everything up or hide your talents and abilities to follow Christ. She was a compassionate and loving mother to all who were in need, but equally ready to give a sharp reprimand to anyone, high or low, who needed to be criticized. A good parent loves unconditionally, but always knows when it's time to say, "No." It's part of human nature to feel lonely, angry, misunderstood, and unappreciated by others at times. And it's very easy to feel justified to wallow in self-pity when life doesn't treat us right. That's the time where we can all use a loving parent in our lives, spiritual or otherwise, to slap us into shape and make us face the reality of finding true satisfaction in helping others rather than always thinking of ourselves. St. Bridget's good example shows us that it's possible to love God, love your neighbor, and still have it all.

JOSEPH OF ARIMATHEA – JULY 31

Joseph was a wealthy, respected member of the Pharisees and a member of the High Council (Sanhedrin) in Jerusalem, a group consisting of leaders from both the Pharisees and the Sadducees. The Pharisees were laymen and very conservative, much like the Puritans. The Sadducees were priests, a hereditary office only available to descendants of Aaron, the brother of Moses. The Sadducees were more liberal than the Pharisees, and they were willing to deal with the Romans and the Herod family.

There is also a British tradition connecting Joseph of Arimathea with England, specifically the Cornwall area of southwestern England. The legend goes that Joseph derived his wealth from the tin mines of Cornwall. Tin, which is an essential ingredient in making bronze, was highly prized in ancient times, and Phoenician ships imported it from Cornwall to the rest of the Roman Empire. It's quite possible that one or more of the investors in the import business could have been Jewish businessmen like Joseph.

After the Crucifixion, or so the legend goes, Joseph went to Cornwall as a missionary, bringing along the chalice that Jesus used at the Last Supper. This chalice is better known to Camelot-lovers as the Holy Grail. When Joseph arrived at the village of Glastonbury (considered by some to be King Arthur's island of Avalon) he planted his walking staff into the ground. It took root and blossomed into a thorn tree. The Holy Thorn Tree still exists on the grounds of Glastonbury Abbey and always blossoms twice a year in the spring and at Christmas. Joseph then dropped the Holy Grail into a well at the foot of Tor Hill, not far from the Abbey. The Holy Grail is said to have turned the water blood red. Chalice Well can also be visited today. It is in a lovely terrace garden, and the well itself is very simple: basically just a cistern with a fancy, Celtic-design manhole cover. The well is opened every day, and the water is still a reddish color, although British scientists say that it's due to the high iron ore content in the water. The Grail itself has never been found.

Since Christianity appears to have gained a foothold in Britain very early, even earlier than Gaul, it may well have been brought there by Christians in the tin trade, so the legend of Joseph's visit to England might have some factual basis. At any rate, it does make a heck of a story. But now back to historical facts....

What we do know from the New Testament is that Joseph publicly asked Pilate for the body of Jesus in order to give him a proper burial, and this is why Joseph of Arimathea is considered the patron saint of undertakers and funeral directors. In Roman times the bodies of criminals who were crucified were either left on the cross to rot away, or else thrown in a common grave pit outside of town. By openly asking permission to bury Jesus, Joseph was making a bold and very brave statement. Through this act everyone in town would know he was a follower of Jesus. He could lose his political and business contacts and his religious position, and consequently lose all his wealth. Joseph of Arimathea had far more to lose then the working-class Apostles who ran away and went into hiding.

It was St. Joseph's great faith that banished all fear. He had it. The women of Jerusalem who stayed at the foot of the Cross had it. But the apostles didn't have that faith until much later, because they were too involved in their own fears. Even today, we sometimes find ourselves wanting to do the right thing, but get caught up in being afraid of what others might say or what others might think. Take a lesson from St. Joseph of Arimathea: fear loses all power when it is replaced by love.

St. Joseph of Arimathea

FRANZ JAGERSTATTER – AUGUST 9

Franz Jagerstatter was born in 1907 in the small town of St. Radegund, Austria. After his natural father was killed in World War I, his mother married a farmer named Jagerstatter who adopted little Franz. After gaining a reputation as a rather wild young man, Franz married and settled down to a typical peasant. In addition to his farm and family duties, Franz became the sexton of his parish church, and was known for his diligent and devout service.

He also became known for his opposition to the Nazi regime. He felt that Hitler, the Nazi government and the war were all immoral. When Franz was called to active duty in the military in 1943, he sought counsel from his parish priest, then the priest in the next village, and finally the bishop of the diocese. Each assured him that this military service was compatible with his Christianity and he could serve with a clear conscience. Franz then reported to the induction center but told them as a conscientious objector he could not serve. The penalty at that time for refusing to serve in the army was death by beheading.

The local draft board felt sorry for the poor, young, deluded farmer, so they got him a military lawyer who managed to get Franz a job offer as a non-combatant medic. But Franz turned down the offer. His felt that if he was in the medical corps and wore the Nazi uniform, it would imply consent to Hitler and the war. His lawyer pointed out that no Austrian or German bishop in any sermon or pastoral letter had ever called on Roman Catholics to refuse military service or oppose the war effort. And that there were millions of patriotic Austrian and German Christians who had no problems with their consciences. When asked why no one but Franz seemed to have such a problem, he replied, "Perhaps they do not have the grace to see it, but I do have the grace to see it, and so I cannot serve."

Franz was sent to prison in Berlin, convicted in a military trial, and executed on August 9, 1943. He was survived by his wife and three small daughters, the eldest of whom was only six. He also left behind a collection of essays and letters from prison.

The moral question at the time was the choice of formal evil (such as shooting someone) versus material cooperation with evil (merely selling someone a gun). The priests and bishop (and indeed most Christian leaders in Germany and Austria at the time) felt that by joining the army and serving his country, Franz was not being asked to commit a sin. If he refused, they would just get another recruit, and if he still refused, they would kill him. So the church leaders told Franz that he was morally absolved and should obey the government, and that is what millions of people, most of them Christians, did under Hitler's regime. Only a small percentage, like the Lutheran minister Dietrich Bonhoeffer, the Franciscan friar Maximilian Kolbe, and a few thousand more were imprisoned or executed for refusing to cooperate. Adolf Hitler was able to plunge the world into war and kill an estimated 6 million Jews, not because the other 30 million Germans agreed, but because they felt they couldn't make a difference, they were just doing their jobs, and were therefore not responsible for the evil they helped create.

"Martyr" is the Greek word for "witness." St. Franz was not trying to be a martyr for a political cause. He was simply doing what he knew he had to do: to refuse to cooperate with evil, to bear witness to Christ, and, if necessary, to pay the ultimate price for that commitment. He knew that his faith was all about witness – a willingness to lose everything he had: his wife, his children, and even his life, rather than give up his belief in the message of Christ.

Risking all for the love of Christ: for us today it's not imprisonment and death. Perhaps it's the risk of ridicule from our family and friends if we say we're going to church on Sunday, the risk of people thinking we're "weird," the risk of reaching out to someone and having them refuse and reject our efforts. But isn't that part of being a Christian? We knew the job was dangerous when we took it. In one of his last letters to his wife from prison, St. Franz explained why the risk was worth all the effort, in words that still ring true today.

"Just as the man who thinks only of this world does everything possible to make life here easier and better, so must we, too, convince ourselves that our struggle is for the eternal Kingdom. But with this difference: we need no rifles or pistols for our battle, but instead, spiritual weapons – and the foremost among these is prayer."

"Let us love our enemies, bless those who curse us, pray for those who persecute us. For love will conquer and will endure for all eternity. And happy are we who live and die, if we must, in God's love."

MARY THE VIRGIN MOTHER OF CHRIST – AUGUST 15

The tendency of some religious traditions to make a "goddess" out of St. Mary the Virgin Mother of Christ does her a great disservice. She did not have a divine life, free from human drudgery, illness, hard times, or sorrow. The Holy Family didn't live like the old television show "Bewitched" where miracles saved the day in every domestic crisis.

Our Mary was a hard-working mother and wife who raised children, was widowed, and watched her oldest son's public execution. But she was also standing by after His Resurrection, and she was there when the Holy Spirit came down at Pentecost. I think it's a wonderful concept to see her as a loving Jewish mother proudly proclaiming, "This is my son, my baby, and I'm so proud of Him! But He is also the Son of God."

If Mary is seen as a almost-divine creature, far above all other mortals, we lose her example of human love, compassion, self-sacrifice, and nobility. If she is deified, the ultimate lesson for us "poor banished children of Eve" is that only superhumans can ever hope to truly follow Christ. The rest of us unworthy sinners can only show up for church, donate money, and hope and pray for the best here and in the hereafter.

One of the greatest stories in the New Testament is the description of the wedding feast at Cana where Jesus performed His

Calling More Saints

St. Mary

MARY THE VIRGIN MOTHER OF CHRIST – AUGUST 15

The tendency of some religious traditions to make a "goddess" out of St. Mary the Virgin Mother of Christ does her a great disservice. She did not have a divine life, free from human drudgery, illness, hard times, or sorrow. The Holy Family didn't live like the old television show "Bewitched" where miracles saved the day in every domestic crisis.

Our Mary was a hard-working mother and wife who raised children, was widowed, and watched her oldest son's public execution. But she was also standing by after His Resurrection, and she was there when the Holy Spirit came down at Pentecost. I think it's a wonderful concept to see her as a loving Jewish mother proudly proclaiming, "This is my son, my baby, and I'm so proud of Him! But He is also the Son of God."

If Mary is seen as a almost-divine creature, far above all other mortals, we lose her example of human love, compassion, self-sacrifice, and nobility. If she is deified, the ultimate lesson for us "poor banished children of Eve" is that only superhumans can ever hope to truly follow Christ. The rest of us unworthy sinners can only show up for church, donate money, and hope and pray for the best here and in the hereafter.

One of the greatest stories in the New Testament is the description of the wedding feast at Cana where Jesus performed His first miracle of changing water into wine. But I think what we also have here is the story of a boy and his mom. The bride and groom may well have been related to Jesus and Mary, and all the apostles were invited as well. Wedding feasts in those days were a 3-day-weekend kind of affair where the families of the married couple provided food, drink and lodging for all the guests if they could afford it, and obviously the family at Cana was well-to-do. Mary heard that the wine had run out in the middle of the celebration, and realized that this would be a major embarrassment for the young couple. So she seeks out her son and tells Him that they have no wine, suggesting she knows He has the power to do something about the situation. Jesus' reply in the Gospel seems a little distant and curt: "Woman, what has that to do with me? My hour has not yet come." But any guy knows that what Jesus really said was probably close to "Come on, Ma... I'm here with the guys! We're here to have a good time, not to start something. Just forget about it!"

But this mother knows her son. She knows the time to start His public life has arrived and He will accept the challenge, even if He wants to avoid it at first. I think the interaction between Jesus and Mary is an example of tough love in action. Jesus is not sure He is ready to make a public statement, but Mary knows He needs a firm push in the right direction to get Him started. It's as if she is telling Him, "Son, I know you have doubts but the moment has arrived. If not you, than who? If not now, when?"

I believe Mary's message to us is best told in her command to the servants: "Listen to my son. Do whatever He tells you." In essence she is saying to all of us, "Don't look at me in adoration. Look to Jesus. He is the one true Light of the World. I just reflect a little of His light and His love, and all of you have the power to do the same. So listen to your mother: don't worship me. Let's go together and follow Him."

Calling More Saints

St. Mary

AUGUSTINE OF HIPPO – AUGUST 28

Augustine was born in the city of Tagaste (near modern Tunis in North Africa) in 354, son of a pagan father and a now famous Christian mother, St. Monica. As a child, Monica had instructed him in the Christian religion and taught him to pray; falling dangerously ill, he desired baptism and his mother got everything ready for it, but he suddenly grew better, and it was put off.

Augustine went to Carthage towards the end of the year 370, in the beginning of his seventeenth year. He was a gifted student and became an expert in rhetoric (public speaking and debate). Soon he entered into an affair with a woman he lived with for the next 15 years (she bore him a son, Adeodatus, in 372).

For a long time he was attracted by the teachings of Manicheism (a dualistic philosophy that taught that the universe is the scene of an unending battle between light and darkness, good and evil, knowledge and ignorance, soul and body, etc.), which claimed to be especially suited for the intellectually elite. After meeting the leading Manichean teacher, Faustus, however, he began to be disillusioned about that sect. In 383 Augustine moved to Rome with a bunch of his close friends, his son, and his "significant other" girlfriend, without telling his mother so she wouldn't get the chance to talk him out of it.

He opened a school of rhetoric in Rome, and later received the post of master professor of rhetoric in Milan. Monica finally tracked him down in Milan and moved into his expanding household. Augustine was a big success here and received many high honors.

But his mother never gave up trying to reform him. She convinced Augustine to go to church to meet the local bishop, St. Ambrose. Augustine often went to hear the bishop's sermons, not because he believed in the Christian message, but because he was greatly impressed by Ambrose's reasoning and eloquence as a speaker.

His mistress began pressuring Augustine to make a decision on getting married. Even after being together for 15 years, Augustine still refused to make a commitment. He also considered his common-law wife beneath him intellectually and socially. Augustine truly acted like a bum, a fact he freely admits in his famous autobiography, *Confessions,* which he wrote as a step-by-step guide to breaking bad habits and compulsions. Adeodatus' mother returned to Africa but she left their son behind, knowing that Augustine could provide for him far better than she ever could. Monica now hoped her wayward son would finally settle down to a Christian life, but it was not to be: he started having affairs with all the women he could find. This was the period when Augustine composed his famous prayer, "Lord, give me chastity...but not yet!"

One day a professor friend, who was a Christian, came to visit Augustine and his friends. Finding a book of St. Paul's epistles lying on the table, he told the gang about the life of St. Antony the Desert Father, and was surprised to find that Augustine and friends had never heard of him or the monastic lifestyle. After his friend had gone, Augustine found himself torn between the memories of his former sins versus the philosophy of Christian service for others. At that point he heard the voice of a child singing from a neighboring house, "Tolle lege! Tolle lege!" ("Take up and read! Take up and read!"). He opened the book of St. Paul's epistles, and read the words: "Not in rioting and drunkenness and envy; but rather put on the Lord Jesus Christ and put aside the things of the flesh." He shut the book, and told the rest of his friends what had passed. They were all convinced at that moment to join Augustine in becoming Christians. Then all the guys immediately went in and told Monica, who rejoiced and praised God for answering her prayers after 17 years. This was in September of 386 when Augustine was thirty-two.

He gave up his school and retired to a country house near Milan, along with Monica, his brother Navigius, his son Adeodatus, and several other friends, and they lived a community life together. St. Augustine was baptized by St. Ambrose on the Vigil of Easter in 387, together with all his friends and his son, who was about sixteen. In the autumn he decided it was time to return to Africa. He went home with his mother and friends, and St. Monica and his son died there during a fever epidemic later that year.

Augustine lived almost three years with his friends at the family estate in Tagaste, serving God in fasting, prayer, good works, and instructing others by his lectures and books. All things were held in common and were distributed according to everyone's needs, like the early Christians in the Acts of the Apostles. Augustine had no intention of becoming a priest, but in 391 he was ordained as an assistant to Valerius, Bishop of Hippo due to his new-found fame as a religious writer and the personal recommendations of St. Ambrose. So Augustine moved to the city of Hippo not far away, and, in a house adjoining the basilica, he established a sort of monastery modeled on his household at Tagaste, living there with his entourage of faithful friends.

Four years later he was consecrated assistant bishop to Valerius, and succeeded him on his death the following year. Augustine established common life at his basilica, and required all the priests, deacons, and subdeacons that lived with him to renounce property and to follow the version of a monastic rule he established there. This later became the basis of the Augustinian Canons, a religious order where priests and deacons who were assigned to a particular cathedral lived as monks, as opposed to say, Benedictines, who established separate, free-standing monasteries unconnected to a bishop's basilica or cathedral. For instance, Martin Luther started off as an Augustinian monk attached to the Wittenburg Cathedral.

Throughout his thirty-five years as bishop of Hippo, St. Augustine had to defend the Catholic faith against one heresy or another. His book *The City of God* is a reply to those who said that the Roman Empire was falling apart because the Christians had taken over. In it he discusses the work of God in history, and the relation between the Christian as citizen on earth and the Christian as citizen of heaven. He also wrote several other books, and corresponded extensively against the Donatists, a heretical group who believed that a sacrament is only as good as the priest who administers it, so that if you were baptized or married by a sinful priest or bishop, those sacraments were invalid.

St. Augustine wrote that it takes more than just prayers and good intentions to really change your bad habits. You need prayer plus some personal effort to avoid temptation and break from your past. We need to stop thinking only about ourselves, and start thinking of the ways we can serve others in Christ. Augustine felt that it's not enough to recite endless prayers in church, and then have nothing to do with your fellow-man. You can't just say the words; you also need to live those words and share that love with everyone you meet. That's part of the job description of being a Christian. Or as St. Augustine would say, "Learn to change the bad habits of selfish sin into the good habits of sharing the love and joy of Christ."

DAVID OAKERHATER – SEPTEMBER 1

David Oakerhater was born in 1850 in Oklahoma. He became a leader of the Cheyenne Indians there. Chief David led a group of warriors against the United States government in a dispute over Indian land rights. In 1875 he and 27 other Indian leaders were taken prisoner by the U.S. Army and sent to a military post in Florida. There, thanks to the efforts of a concerned Army captain who was an Episcopalian, they learned English and discovered the Christian faith. David and three others decided to become Christians, and after they were released, went north to study for the ministry. David was baptized in Syracuse, New York in 1878 and ordained as a deacon in 1881 when he was 31 years old. When he returned to Oklahoma in 1881, he made a speech to the remaining members of his tribe. "You all know me. You remember that when I led you out to war I went first, and what I told you was true. Now I have been away to the East and I have learned about another captain, the Lord Jesus Christ, and He is my leader. He goes first, and all He tells me is true. I have come back to my people to tell you to go with me now down this new road, a way that makes all for peace."

David continued to work among his people, and founded schools and missions until his death in 1931. He was 81 years old, and had served as a deacon for 50 years. The one sad part of this story is that he may not have served as a deacon that long by choice. He may well have wanted to become a priest, but the Church at that time would not ordain him for several reasons. One may have been that he was a former Cheyenne war chief who had killed American soldiers in battle. Another may have been that he wasn't Caucasian. God forgives all sins, but sometimes human nature may not. But David accepted the decision, and spent the rest of his life serving his people and the Episcopal Church with great love.

The moral of this story is to remember that we don't always have all the answers, and are not the only ones with a direct line to God. That is certainly not the message of Christ in the Gospels. Prejudice can fester and grow in any human institution, and the Church is as susceptible as any other to mistakes and transgressions. We need to rise above our petty differences and family squabbles and look up to God who is Father to us all, and who loves us all equally as heirs and not as step-children. That is why we celebrate the life of our American St. David and should follow his example: where there is hatred and fear in our world, our country, or in our church, let us always sow love.

MOTHER TERESA OF CALCUTTA – SEPTEMBER 5

She was born Agnes Gonxha Bojaxhiu in 1910 of Albanian parents in the town of Skopje, which became part of Yugoslavia after World War I. Agnes joined the Sisters of Loreto at age 18 when she went to the order's motherhouse in Dublin, Ireland, and she took the name Teresa when she took her vows. For 20 years she spent her time teaching in the various schools run by the congregation, ending up as the principal of St. Mary's High School in Calcutta, India.

Her future work and the foundation of the Missionaries of Charity in 1950 was an inspiration that came to her on a train trip in September 1946 from Calcutta to Darjeeling. Sister Teresa was on her way to make her annual retreat. On the train back from Darjeeling, Mother Teresa received what she referred to as "a call within a call." She had a revelation to leave the life of a teaching sister and go to work in the streets. Teresa had to explain to her fellow nuns, her Jesuit spiritual advisor, and to the Archbishop of Calcutta that she felt called by the Holy Spirit to do this unusual work. Then she had to wait 2 more years to get official permission from Rome to leave the Loreto congregation but still continue to live as a nun, continuing her vows of poverty, chastity, and obedience.

On August 16, 1948 Sister Teresa moved to Patna to enroll in a short course in nursing taught by the Medical Missionary Sisters, an American order. At this time she decided to replace her old-fashioned nun's habit with the rough cotton sari of poor Indian women. She wore a small crucifix on her left shoulder fastened with a safety pin, and wore sandals without stockings on her feet. She wanted to be one with the people she was going to serve, and so Sister Teresa applied for and eventually received Indian citizenship that same year. Then on December 21, 1948 she went out, alone, to her new life in the slums. She was 38 years old.

In March 1949, two of her former high school students asked to join her. A Bengali Catholic family gave them a house, and soon 10 more young women joined the sisterhood of Mother Superior Teresa in opening a slum school. On their way to the school each morning, Mother Teresa and her nuns would often pass whole families living in the street, or a lone man or woman lying in the gutter, dying. Mother Teresa rented a set of rooms where the homeless could be fed until death released them or until they found enough strength to return to the streets.

In October 1950 the Missionaries of Charity were organized as a religious society, but limited by Rome to the Archdiocese of Calcutta. As they moved about the streets, the sisters often found abandoned babies in alleys and garbage cans. So Mother Teresa opened a Children's Home next to their convent. Women doctors donated their services and were soon staffing new pediatric clinics in various poor areas.

Within a few years, the Missionaries of Charity increased in numbers and were at work in 59 centers in the city. Mother Teresa had all her sisters take a fourth vow: in addition to poverty, chastity and obedience, the sisters also vowed "to give wholehearted and free service to the poorest of the poor."

By 1965, when the Missionaries of Charity were recognized by Rome as a congregation that could work anywhere in the world, there were 300 sisters, almost all of them Indian. The first overseas invitation came from Venezuela. Mother Teresa sent six of her nuns to start a health clinic. Then a call came from Cardinal Terence Cooke to come to New York. Five sisters came over, including one German sister who was a doctor, and they established their headquarters in Harlem. Then requests came from Egypt, Australia and even the Soviet Union. Mother Teresa's sisters were welcomed from Leningrad to Albania.

On Christmas Eve of 1985, Mother Teresa opened her first Home for the Dying in New York's Greenwich Village. "When I head that people were dying of this terrible new disease, I knew we must do something. I found that the dying were mostly young men, and that some of them were dying in prison." The terrible new disease was AIDS. She opened other hospices in Baltimore, Philadelphia, Washington, Denver, and San Francisco.

Journalists often marveled that the Missionaries of Charity operated 477 centers in over 103 countries in less that 30 years. For Mother Teresa, it was business as usual. "God is indeed overwhelmingly good to us. He answers our needs even before we have voiced them. There is a miracle almost every day."

Things were going so well with vocations for women, that Mother Teresa decided to start two other religious orders: the Missionary Fathers and Brothers of Mercy, and the Co-Workers of Mother Teresa for lay people. She received many honorary degrees and awards including the Ceres Medal of the United Nations Food and Agricultural Organization, the Pope John XXIII Peace Prize, and the Templeton Prize for Progress in Religion. In 1979 when she was 70 years old, she was awarded the Nobel Peace Prize for her work throughout the world.

But her constant work and globe-trotting came with a price. In 1983 she was diagnosed with heart problems and had to use a pacemaker. Several serious illnesses and surgeries followed, but Mother Teresa always seemed to bounce back. Then on the evening of September 5, 1997 she died of a massive heart attack in Calcutta. People around the world who had been touched by the Tiny Dynamo of India all agreed that a great saint had passed from this world to heaven.

But in life, Mother Teresa faced her share of criticism. Some religious leaders in Latin America complained about her caring for the poor without attacking the political structures that trapped them in poverty. Some conservative Christian groups felt that while there was no denying her humanitarian efforts, she may have fallen short as a Christian by not demanding that her hospice patients of different religions accept Jesus Christ and be baptized. Mother Theresa would allow those dying to have the comfort of their particular religion, and if they wanted a Hindu priest, or a Muslim or Sikh or Buddhist to comfort them in their last hours, she would arrange it. She felt that Christ was love, and that anyone, regardless of religious affiliation, who has that love has Christ, and if He decides, that in itself could be a baptism by love. "It's all God's work and God's decision, not mine," she said in an interview. "I am just a little pencil in the hand of God. I simply continue to love Christ in the poor."

Mother Teresa believed that serving Christ meant serving the poor, the hungry, the lonely, and the suffering, regardless of nationality or religious affiliation. She had an answer for what was the greatest problem facing western society today:

"The worst disease today is not leprosy or AIDS. It is being unwanted, being left out, being forgotten. The greatest scourge is to forget the next person, to be so suffocated with things that we have no time for the lonely person, even a person in our own family who needs us."

St. Mother Teresa lived out the beatitude: "Blessed are the merciful." She could be as tenacious as a bulldog, and as gentle and loving as a favorite grandmother. Her legacy of love continues to be an example and a challenge for us all. We can change this world for the better, and we can do it, like her, one person at a time.

JOHN HENRY HOBART – SEPTEMBER 12

After the American Revolution, the Episcopal Church, under public suspicion in many quarters because of its previous association with the Church of England, was very low-key and did very little for about twenty years. John Henry Hobart was one of the men who changed that.

He was born in Philadelphia in 1775, the son of a ship's captain. He was educated at the University of Pennsylvania and graduated from Princeton University in 1793. He decided to enter the church and was ordained a deacon in 1798 and a priest in 1801. He served at several parishes in Pennsylvania, New Jersey, and New York. He showed great ability, and at age 36, was consecrated Assistant Bishop of the Diocese of New York. Five years later, he became the Diocesan (Head Bishop).

As bishop he helped found two institutions of learning: Geneva (later to become Hobart College) and the General Theological Seminary in New York. He not only looked after the Diocese of New York (46,000 square miles at the time and virtual wilderness west and north of Albany) but also served as the rector of Trinity Parish, the wealthiest and most influential church in the country. He also looked after the Dioceses of Connecticut and New Jersey, who were without bishops at the time.

To look at Bishop John, you probably wouldn't have thought you were looking at a great leader. He was short, nearsighted, and had to wear thick, Benjamin Franklin-style spectacles. In an age of subtle gestures in the pulpit, he was sometimes melodramatic. At a time of dignified public speaking, he spoke rapidly with emotion. When most men were reserved, even with their families, he was warm, whether with financiers or farmers, to the point of being thought odd. In other words, he would hug people a lot and talk about love, things you just didn't do back in those days, especially not in church. Actually, this is very much how I act at St. James in South Pasadena, but that's another story.

Bishop John was also one of the first leaders in the church to publish theological and devotional manuals specifically for lay people, especially those without higher education. He wanted the poor as well as the rich to have a religious education to enrich their daily lives. It was said that even those who disagreed with some of his ideas and his preaching style respected his great faith and personal integrity. His love for Christ was clearly seen in all that he did for the people he served. May the same be said of all of us today. Now go out there and hug someone the next time you're in church!

SERGIUS OF RUSSIA – SEPTEMBER 25

He was born into a middle-class Russian family in 1314 and baptized with the name Bartholomew. His family lost everything in a civil war between Moscow and Rostov when he was 15. Forced to flee the city, Bartholomew's family moved to Radonezh, about 50 miles north of Moscow. Here they lived as peasant farmers, working the fields for local land-owners.

Five years later, Bartholomew and his brother, Stephen, decided to become hermit monks in the forest outside of town. They built a log cabin and a tiny wooden church dedicated to the Holy Trinity. Stephen decided he couldn't stand the rough winters, so he left the hermit life. But Bartholomew liked the simple life.

He asked a local abbot to accept his profession as a monk, and this is when he took the name of Sergius. He had intended to stay as a solitary monk, but his reputation as a wise man brought him lots of visitors. More monks wanted to join up with Sergius as their abbot, and the Monastery of Holy Trinity that grew up around that first little church became a major pilgrimage site for all those seeking spiritual instruction, advice, and encouragement.

In 1380, Prince Dimitri Donskoy of Moscow consulted Sergius before a battle against Tartar invaders. Sergius predicted that if the Russian troops would pray and fight for God and their country, they would be victorious, and so he made speeches to rally the people to get behind the prince. It wasn't long before Dimitri and his men had the support of the Russian people, the Tartars were finally defeated, and Sergius became a national hero.

Now Sergius devoted his time to bringing peace to all Russia by reconciling rival princes and noblemen. In 1378 he refused the honor of becoming Patriarch of Moscow saying, "Since the days of my youth, I have never worn gold. Now that I am an old man, more than ever I must adhere to my poverty in Christ." By the time he died in 1382 he had founded 40 monasteries throughout Russia. Pilgrims still visit his shrine at the monastery at Zagorsk, the city that is the official residence of the Patriarch of Moscow.

Sergius was known as a kind and gentle monk who remained close to the peasant lifestyle. Legends about his love for animals gave him the reputation as the St. Francis of Assisi of Russia. He was a hard-working abbot, equally at home working the fields along side the Radonezh peasants as he was in giving spiritual advice to the Russian nobility in the monastery chapel.

Although his animal stories and his leadership in the quest for Russian independence have gained him a place in history, St. Sergius would be the first to say his most important job was to inspire others to know God's love and to show them how to respond to that love by sharing it with others. It's a job description that we, as Christians, would do well to match in our own lives today.

St. Sergius of Russia

TERESA OF AVILA – OCTOBER 15

Teresa de Cepeda y Ahumada (later known as Teresa de Jesus) was born in Avila, Spain in 1515, one of 10 children. Her family was of part Jewish ancestry, and her mother died when she was 15. Teresa decided she wanted to become a nun, and when she was 20, she entered the local Carmelite convent. While still a novice she fell seriously ill, was in coma for a while, and ended up partially paralyzed for 3 years. Her prayer life deepened as a result of her long illness, and she began to have visions and a vivid sense of the presence of God in her life.

After she recovered in 1560, Teresa decided to attempt to reform the rules of her convent, which she considered to have strayed from the Carmelites' original intent. At that time, many wealthy widows and the daughters of influential families became nuns for the social prestige and position. They were more like fancy sorority houses and literary salons where visitors came and social gatherings took place. Teresa felt such things had gotten totally out of hand. Her proposed reforms included strict enclosure, meaning the nuns were not to leave the convent to attend parties and that such social events at the convent would be forbidden. The nuns were to remain in the convent to pray and study, and must become "discalced," which literally meant "going barefoot." To Teresa this symbolized a life of poverty, humility, and the simple life, unburdened by luxury and the other distractions of high society.

In 1562 she received permission from the Carmelite Order to open a new convent in Avila, much to the anger and opposition of the town and patrons of the older convent. But her reform movement proved successful, and she was allowed to travel throughout Spain establishing 17 houses of "Carmelites of the Strict Observance." All her convents were small, poor, and strictly enclosed. Teresa became close friends with St. John of the Cross, another Carmelite mystic and author, who was influenced by her to establish similar reforms among the Carmelite friars.

Teresa is said to have been very attractive in appearance, as well as funny and affectionate. She was as famous for her achievements in organizing religious communities as she was for her writings on contemplative prayer. She wrote an autobiography, several books on meditation, and a collection of 31 poems and letters. St. Teresa of Avila also has the distinction of being one of only two women to be named Doctors of the Church for their profound theological insight and wisdom (St. Catherine of Siena, from my first book, *CALLING ALL SAINTS*, is the other).

Teresa believed that while contemplative prayer and time spent alone is essential for the Christian life, God must not be removed from the everyday events of our lives. He shouldn't be treated like good china, worshipped on special occasions only (like Christmas, Easter, and Sunday mornings), but then packed up for the rest of the week. One of her poems describes her feeling that we are the only means that God has to share His love with others in our day-to-day world.

> "Christ has no body now but yours,
> No hand, no feet on earth but yours.
> Yours are the eyes through which He looks compassion on this world.
> Christ has no body now on earth but yours."

It is through our example and the actions of our daily lives that others will see, or fail to see, how a Christian acts, loves, shares, and helps others. If we don't walk the walk, how can we expect anyone to make the effort?

Shortly before her death, St. Teresa wrote a poem on a bookmark in her prayerbook that sums up her message for us in a world that is as troubled and turbulent as her own. May it remind us of the serenity that is possible when we take the time to listen to that small, still voice in our hearts.

> "Let nothing disturb you, nothing cause you fear;
> All things pass. God is unchanging.
> Patience obtains all:
> Whoever has God needs nothing else; God alone suffices."

St. Teresa of Avila

MARTIN OF TOURS - NOVEMBER 11

Martin was born in Italy around 330 AD. His father was a decorated military veteran, and he demanded that Martin enlist in the army at the age of 15, even though Martin didn't want a military career. But Martin, like his father, showed definite leadership abilities, and was soon promoted up the ranks while serving in Gaul. One winter's day while on patrol, Martin saw a old beggar at the city gate of Amiens. Martin had no money to give, and when his fellow soldiers refused to help the old man, Martin cut his officer's cloak in two and gave half to the beggar. That same night, Martin had a dream of Christ wearing that same half-cloak and saying, "Martin has covered me with this garment." Martin had for some time considered becoming a Christian, and feeling this was a sign from God, he was soon baptized.

Near the end of his enlistment period, Martin asked to resign from the army saying, "I have faithfully served Caesar, but now I must serve Christ." His general accused him of cowardice because of his Christian pacifism, so Martin offered to stand unarmed between the two armies in the next battle. He wasn't taken up on his offer but instead was sent to the stockade. He was released soon after when peace was signed, and was given the equivalent of an honorable discharge.

Martin studied under St. Hilary of Poitiers, a famous theologian of the time, and eventually founded the first monastery in Gaul. In 371 Martin was elected Bishop of Tours, another promotion that he very reluctantly accepted. He had wished to remain a simple monk leading a quiet life of prayer, but once elected, he handled the job with military efficiency. The people in the area were mainly pagans at the time, but his kindness, sound teaching, and good example brought many people to Christ. In one instance, some Druid priests agreed to cut down their sacred idol, a giant fir tree, if St. Martin would agree to stand directly in its path. Always ready to accept a challenge, Bishop Martin instantly agreed, and the tree narrowly missed him. This was enough to convince all the Druids in the area to convert to Christianity and be baptized.

He remained a staunch defender of the poor and helpless, and made annual visits to every parish, monastery, and convent in his large diocese by foot, by donkey, or by boat, depending on the terrain. After many years of service to his people, Martin died in November of 397. His shrine at Tours became a major pilgrimage stop during the Middle Ages.

St. Martin's feast day of November 11 is also our Veterans Day. It was originally known as Armistice Day to mark the end of World War I, but was later changed to honor the veterans of all wars. I think that makes it the perfect day to honor St. Martin, the soldier who fought bravely and faithfully in the military, and then re-enlisted in the service of Christ.

HUGH OF LINCOLN – NOVEMBER 17

Hugh was born in Burgundy, France around 1140. His parents were well known for their faith and works of charity. Hugh decided to join the Carthusian Order of monks, and so impressed his superiors that he was appointed procurator of the monastery in 1173. As procurator he was in charge of all business affairs, guest services, and distribution of food and money to the poor. Hugh was very fond of animals, and there are legends about his adventures with animals very similar to those of St. Francis of Assisi. Birds and squirrels would eat out of his hand, and he had a swan that served as a watch dog. It would follow him around and keep guard over his bed at night, so that no one could approach Hugh without permission for fear of being attacked by his infamous watch-swan.

As a sign of penance for his role in the murder of the Archbishop Thomas Becket, King Henry II decided to found the first Carthusian monastery in Somerset, England. Difficulties arose with the first two priors, and the French government recommended Hugh. He arrived in England in 1176 and immediately engaged in clashes with Henry. For instance, Hugh refused to take up his duties as prior of the monastery until Henry reimbursed the peasants whose land had been seized to build it. "I do not despair of you," Hugh said to him at their first interview; "Even though I know how much your many occupations interfere with the health of your soul." Henry, impressed by his attitude, swore that while he lived he should never leave his kingdom, and took so much pleasure in his conversation and his counsel that a rumor arose that Hugh was his illegitimate son. Hugh's biographer wrote that "of all men only Hugh could bend that rhinoceros, Henry, to his will."

In 1186 Hugh was also made Bishop of Lincoln. He arrived at his own consecration wearing his oldest monk's habit and riding on a mule, much to the embarrassment of all the knights, bishops, and other leaders who attended. After the ceremony, Hugh hosted a great feast to which all the poor of Lincoln were invited. He took a stern view of the ill-treatment of the poor by the royalty and the clergy, since he saw any injustice to the poor as a crime against God. He began a series of social welfare programs to feed the poor, protect outcasts, and heal the sick. It was said he was responsible for many miraculous cures.

The outcasts of the day that most caught his attention were the 2,000 Jews living in England at the end of the 12th Century. They were considered the king's serfs: their property was the king's and they lived under his protection, confined to ghettos and only permitted certain occupations, like money-lending. But when King Henry died, the royal protection ended. Riots broke out against the Jews in many areas. At the time of the Crusades, when Richard the Lion-Hearted was king, hostilities increased against the Jews who were now attacked as "enemies of the Cross."

In defense of the persecuted Jews, Hugh faced armed mobs in Lincoln, Stratford and Northampton, standing between them and their intended Jewish victims. This was hardly the politically correct thing to do at the time, but Hugh stood firm, unafraid of the personal consequences. He shamed the mobs and compelled them to submit to his demand for peace between Christians and non-Christians.

When St. Hugh died, the entire Jewish ghetto of Lincoln turned out to mourn him at his funeral along with bishops, abbots, kings, princes and commoners. It was said that lamentations were made in every street by Christians and Jews alike for "the true servant indeed of the great God." Pilgrims visited his shrine in great numbers and many miraculous cures were reported.

St. Hugh, following the example of Christ, felt the need to stand up for the outcasts of society. Whether they were the poor, the uneducated, the weak, or the different, he felt the call of Christ to reach out, to love, and to make things better. His courage in defending the Jews can be compared to those Christians in World War II who faced danger to protect them from the Nazi Holocaust. St. Hugh's example makes us wonder if perhaps the Holocaust itself could have been prevented if more bishops and other church leaders had been willing to stand up against the evils of the Third Reich.

Sometimes we have to be willing to stand up and do the right thing, in spite of the consequences, in the office, in the schoolyard, and in our own neighborhoods when we see injustice being done. Being a Christian can be tough sometimes, but we knew the job was potentially dangerous when we took it. But only by taking risks, like St. Hugh, can we reach our ultimate goal of becoming "true servants indeed of the great God."

HILDA OF WHITBY – NOVEMBER 18

Hilda was the grandniece of King Edwin of Northumbria. She was born in 614 and baptized at age 13 when the king and his entire household became Christians. When she was 33, Hilda felt a call to leave court and enter religious life. She had planned to enter a convent in France, but St. Aidan, the bishop of Northumbria, convinced her that God had special plans for her in England. He appointed her the abbess of a new convent at Hartlepool and she was a great success.

Her most famous achievement came a few years later, when she left Hartlepool to establish a new monastery at Whitby. It was a double monastery: one community of men and another of women, with the chapel in between, and Hilda as the abbess over both. It became the center of English learning, and St. Hilda is often considered the "mother" of English literature. Books were highly prized at Whitby, and nuns and monks both worked at copying manuscripts, using parchment and inks that were made on site.

Abbesses in the medieval church were in such high esteem for their learning, sanctity, and wisdom that they participated in all church councils. Their names followed bishops (but came before priests and monks) as signatures on official documents. In fact, abbesses in those days were consecrated by bishops and received a bishop's crosier (staff) and miter (hat) as symbols of their power. The ladies in question had no sacramental or ordination powers, and they didn't actually wear the miter, but it was carried before them on a cushion at all official church events. If you examine medieval paintings and stained-glass windows, you will always see an abbess saint depicted holding a bishop's crosier as her symbol of rank.

The Celtic people of Britain had heard the Gospel well before 300 AD, but after the Romans left, a massive invasion of Germanic peoples (Angles and Saxons) forced the native Celts out of England and into Wales, Ireland, and Scotland. Celtic missionaries (like Saints Brendan and Columba) went to the north and west, and other missionaries (like St. Augustine of Canterbury) were sent by Rome to the south and east of England.

Roman and Celtic traditions differed, not so much in doctrine, but on such questions as the correct date to celebrate Easter and the proper style of tonsure for monks and other clergy. The Roman style was to shave the head except for a crown of hair (what we consider the typical "Friar Tuck" hairstyle). But the Celtic monks always shaved their heads in front from ear to ear, and let their hair grow long in back, not unlike male-pattern baldness.

Other disagreements concerned whether or not the church should own property and raise money to build large cathedrals (a Roman custom) or follow a simple lifestyle and serve the common people (the Celtic version of religious life). During Hilda's time it became clear that the English church would have to choose between the old Celtic customs and the customs of Rome. It was as an honor to Hilda that her monastery was chosen to be the site of the Synod of Whitby in 664 to consider the matter, and it was decided after much not-always-friendly debate to follow the Roman customs throughout England.

Hilda herself greatly preferred the Celtic customs, but once the decision was made, she used her influence to get others to accept the Roman ways peacefully. Her influence was considerable because she was also considered the wisest woman in England by kings and commoners alike. She died at Whitby on November 17, 680. Her last words to her monks and nuns gathered around her were, "Love one another: it is the greatest Christian virtue."

A woman of great devotion and ecclesiastical ability, St. Hilda was a major influence on the Celtic church in Ireland, Scotland, England and Wales throughout the 7th Century. Her prudence and good sense gained her the respect of every bishop in Great Britain, and she was considered by them to be their equal. In these days of continuing debate about what is or isn't the proper role for women in business, social, political, and religious life, it's nice to remember that God has always been an equal opportunity employer. St. Hilda of Whitby proves that a woman in a position of power and influence, combined with a strong sense of justice and love, can be a leader and role model for us all.

FRANCIS XAVIER – DECEMBER 3

Francis Xavier, or Francisco do Yasu y Javier, was born in 1506, the youngest son of a prominent Basque family from northern Spain. When he was 18 he studied at the University of Paris, where he met Ignatius Loyola and joined together with him and five others in the service of God by forming the Society of Jesus (better known as the Jesuits) in 1534. He and another priest were sent by Ignatius on the Society's first missionary expedition to the East Indies.

First stop was Lisbon, Portugal where they were supposed to board a ship to take them to India. However, King John II of Portugal liked the two Jesuits so much that he arranged for them to say in town for a whole year, serving as priests to the royal court. Francis' companion, Father Simon Rodriquez, liked it so much he got permission to stay on permanently, but Francis was anxious to get moving. So on April 7, 1541, his 35th birthday, Francis was commissioned by the King as apostolic nuncio for the East Indies, which happened to be under Portuguese control at the time.

Francis set sail with two other Jesuits who were sent as his new assistants. It was a long voyage with a lot of delays due to bad weather. They finally arrived at Goa, a Portuguese colony on the west coast of India. Francis began learning the language and writing a catechism for the instruction of converts. Since most of the working people were illiterate, he got the idea of writing lyrics about the Christian faith to the music of popular songs. His "Christ Tunes" became instant hits among the people and were sung everywhere.

He also visited the prisons and the hospitals, conducted worship services among the lepers, and walked the streets ringing a bell to call the children for religious instruction. Francis found that the Portuguese settlers and soldiers of the colony were brutal in their treatment of the natives, and that their manner of life hardly recommended the value of the Christian faith to any non-believers. But Francis was up to the challenge. He preached tirelessly, both to the native peoples and to all the Europeans living there.

Francis spent the next 10 years traveling throughout India and Malaysia. He did have the valuable insight to adjust to the likes and dislikes of the diverse cultures he encountered, which helped him succeed where other European missionaries had failed. His friendly personality and genuine concern for the poor and suffering made him recognizable to all as a holy man who deserved respect.

While working in Malaysia, Francis met a Japanese convert named Anjiro who got him interested in a missionary trip to Japan. After a brief return to Goa, he set out for Japan with a Jesuit priest, Anjiro, and two other Japanese converts. Here he learned the language, wrote a catechism, and preached. After limited success, Francis realized that religious poverty was not respected in Japan as it was in India. The idea of a holy man who lived like a beggar was no different than a low-class bum to the Japanese. They respected philosophers and scholars. So Francis decided to change his whole approach. He got himself a black philosopher's kimono, dressed his assistants as attendants, and got an audience with the *daimyo*, the local ruler of the large city of Yamaguchi. Francis introduced himself as the representative of the King of Portugal and presented gifts (a music box, a clock, and a pair of gold spectacles) given to him by the Portuguese authorities in India for just such an occasion. Francis and his gifts made a big impression on the *daimyo*, who gave the Jesuits permission to teach and hold religious services. He even gave them the use of an empty Buddhist monastery for a church residence. With this royal seal of approval, Francis and his missionary team were very successful in that part of Japan over the next three years.

Then Francis returned to Goa where he planned his next challenge: bringing the Gospel to China, which at that time was closed to all foreigners. In August 1552 he bribed a ship's captain to smuggle him into the country. This voyage was also plagued with bad weather. After many delays, Francis landed on an island six miles off the coast of China. While trying to arrange for another ship to take him to the mainland, Francis was stricken with fever and died on December 3, 1552.

Although raised in a wealthy, high-society family, St. Francis made serving the poor, the ignorant, and the unwanted his full-time occupation. Their care and education was his vocation. Like another saint in India some 400 years later, Mother Teresa of Calcutta, Francis Xavier was completely dedicated to the idea that his personal talents and abilities were a gift to be shared with those most in need of love and care, not just to gain him wealth, power, and comfort in the courts of the rich and famous.

In a letter to St. Ignatius, his Jesuit boss, St. Francis once wrote:

"Again and again I have thought of going around the universities of Europe, especially Paris, and crying out to the scholars: 'What a tragedy: how many in the world are never touched by Christ's words of love and compassion, because of you!' This thought would certainly stir most of them to listen actively to what God is saying to them. They would forget their own desires and give themselves over entirely to God's will and his choice. They would cry out with all their heart: 'Lord, here am I! Send me. Send me anywhere you like -- even to India!'"

It's not enough these days to sit back and just hope and pray for a better tomorrow. You have to do something. Volunteer your time. Be part of a literacy program to teach children or adults. Help out at a hospital or senior center. Give some of your time to your local school or library. You don't have to travel to faraway lands to make a difference. You can change the world in your own hometown. Just follow the lead of St. Francis Xavier: "Here I am, Lord. Send me!"

EUSEBIUS OF VERCELLI – DECEMBER 16

Eusebius was born in Sardinia in the early 4th Century. His family moved to Rome, and Eusebius was ordained a lector, one of the minor orders in the church below deacon. When the city of Vercelli was large enough to have its own bishop, Eusebius, who was well known throughout the area as a wise and saintly man, was quickly elected. In those days bishops were still elected by popular vote by the people and the local clergy, so Eusebius went from lector to priest to bishop in a few quick and easy steps.

After becoming a bishop, Eusebius decided to set up a rule of life for all the clergy working and living at his cathedral, and so is considered the founder of the "canon regular" form of religious life. Canon regulars were clergy who were part of a bishop's household, lived under a common rule like monks, and owned no private property. The main difference between a canon regular and a monk was that a monk didn't have to be a priest, but a canon regular was always ordained. St. Augustine of Hippo built upon Eusebius' original concept when he started his own religious order of canons in North Africa at the end of the 4th Century.

Pope Liberius had also noticed Bishop Eusebius' leadership abilities. When Emperor Constantius II convened the Council of Milan in 355, Eusebius was sent to help speak against the Arian heresy. Arianism was a 4th century philosophy based on the writings of Arius, a priest from Alexandria. His basic idea was that Christ was not divine, neither is the Holy Spirit, and so there is no Trinity. God the Father is the only true God. Jesus is a perfect being begotten by God, above all other creatures, but still only a created being. Arius also taught that the Holy Spirit was begotten by Christ, and was inferior to both the Father and Son. In 325 the Council of Nicaea condemned Arianism as a heresy, but it still gained followers among the nobility, generals, senators, and some influential bishops in the church. Emperor Constantine had defended the Council's decrees against this heresy, but when he died, the empire was divided between his sons, Constantus (who ruled in the west and supported the Nicene bishops) and Constantius II (who ruled the eastern part of the Empire and supported Arianism).

The Council of Milan was supposed to be a peace council between the Arians and the rest of the church. Unfortunately, due to political pressures, it turned into a blanket condemnation of all Arian opponents, especially St. Athanasius, who was the leader of the Nicene, God-as-Trinity position. The Arian Constantius tried to force Eusebius and two other non-Arian bishops to condemn Athanasius under pain of death, but the three bishops refused. When the council ended, the Arians had won the day, but the emperor was persuaded to commute the sentence from death to permanent exile in Scythopolis, Palestine.

Once Eusebius was on the enemies list, he was subject to beatings, occasional imprisonment, and other humiliations because his church views were now considered unpatriotic by the new Arian majority. His ill treatment didn't end until 361 when Constantius died and Emperor Julian took the throne. Julian pardoned all the exiled bishops, including Eusebius, and he was finally allowed to return home to Italy. He became good friends with Bishop Hilary of Poitiers (the mentor of St. Martin of Tours), who encouraged Eusebius to become a writer. He wrote a series of books that explained the Church's views on the nature of the Trinity – God the Father, God the Son (Jesus Christ), and God the Holy Spirit – and how they are three distinct Persons, yet remain one God. He died of natural causes in Vercelli in 371.

St. Eusebius didn't do things just because they were expedient or politically correct at the time. He was willing to stand up for his beliefs, even at great personal sacrifice. He could be described as a living martyr for the faith within the "faith," at a time when Arianism almost replaced Christianity as an official religion. In these days of morality based on marketing surveys, and business results being considered more important than personal integrity, it's good to have somebody like St. Eusebius as a role model. He shows us that, even today, some things in heaven and on earth are still worth working and praying and sacrificing for. So remember St. Eusebius: when the going gets tough...just keep the faith and hold on.

THOMAS BECKET – DECEMBER 29

Thomas was born in London in 1118. He was educated at Merton Priory in Surrey, and later in Paris. Thomas' first job was as a clerk to a London merchant, but he soon managed to land the assignment as clerk and secretary to Theobald, the Archbishop of Canterbury. Being an ambitious young man, Thomas ingratiated himself with the old Archbishop, who was so impressed with his abilities that he ordained Thomas to the position of archdeacon of Canterbury, and sent him to Rome several times on important missions.

It wasn't that Thomas had any desire to become a priest. His career interests were in politics, not religion. It was customary in those days for most scholars, whether students or professors, to take minor orders in the Church as a routine part of their education. For Thomas, being archdeacon was a civil service position, not a religious one.

He had a natural talent for administration combined with great charm, energy, and a taste for the good life, and through his work with the court, he came to the notice of King Henry II. Thomas was always looking for good food, good wine, and pretty women, and since the young king shared these same interests, the two became best friends. When an opening came up in 1154, Henry, with the Archbishop's recommendation, appointed Thomas the Chancellor of England.

When Archbishop Theobald died in 1161, Henry wanted to elect Thomas to that position as well. The archbishop had control over all church money, taxes, and lands, and the king thought it was high time to have someone who would understand and obey his wishes as both chancellor and head churchman. Thomas did not want the job at first. He felt he was unworthy of a church leadership position, a feeling shared by all the other English bishops who thought old Theobald had shown far too much favoritism to the upstart former archdeacon. Then Cardinal Henry of Pisa, the papal legate to England, stepped in. He saw in Thomas a depth of character that would be an asset to the Church in England, and told the bishops that since Thomas Becket was favored by God and the Pope, they must agree to the choice.

And so it came to pass that the former archdeacon of Canterbury was ordained a priest on the Saturday after Whitsunday in 1162, and consecrated Archbishop of Canterbury the very next day. Against Henry's objections, Thomas did resign as chancellor in order to devote himself completely to his church work.

Now Henry felt he had what he always wanted: complete control over clergy and church revenues, with his best friend in charge. But the king had badly misjudged Thomas. Becoming archbishop had an profound effect on his best friend's way of life. To everyone's surprise, the fun-loving Thomas started acting like a real servant of God, living an austere life, and putting the interests of the church over the interest of politics. His new way of thinking caused him to clash repeatedly with Henry over the rights of the king and his nobles over the commoners and the church. The king felt hurt, outraged and betrayed. Thomas was forced into exile in France for a while, while Henry tried to officially remove him as Archbishop of Canterbury.

Thomas appealed to Rome, and the pope decided to put his full support behind Archbishop Thomas. He returned to Canterbury in triumph with crowds of people lining the roads and cheering for the faithful archbishop. Several bishops still hated Thomas from the old days and they sided with the king, trying to get Thomas banished from England forever. Finally the fight between king and archbishop reached the breaking point. Henry was at a banquet with several noblemen when the dinner conversation turned to the saga of the ungrateful archbishop who was disobedient to the wishes of his king.

"Can no one rid me of this upstart priest!" shouted Henry to no one in particular. But four knights listened, and decided to take matters into their own hands. They made a plan to ride to Canterbury and silence the troublesome archbishop once and for all.

News of the plan leaked out, and word was sent to Thomas by friends at court, but he refused to run away. While at prayer with his monks in the cathedral, the four knights broke in and stabbed him to death at the foot of the high altar. The king was broken-hearted to think that his words spoken in haste and anger had actually come true. The four conspirators were tried and executed, and King Henry did penance by being publicly whipped at the tomb of Thomas Becket in Canterbury Cathedral. Thomas was soon proclaimed a saint, and his shrine became a major pilgrimage designation. Remember that group of medieval travelers described in Chaucer's *Canterbury Tales*? The book is a collection of the stories they tell to pass the time on their journey across England to the shrine of St. Thomas.

It is interesting to note that Thomas could have escaped. He knew the knights were coming and that his life was in danger. Instead, he stood his ground and did not attempt to fight back. Thomas Becket had found a cause that he considered worth dying for. He felt he was "saving God's honor" by his stand against the King, not unlike the situation another St. Thomas (More) found himself in with another Henry (VIII) four hundred years later.

St. Thomas was a man of great pride and ambition, but he stood up against the cultural and financial pressures of his privileged life to defend the rights of the common people. He refused to take the easy way out. May we, like St. Thomas, have the courage to stand up to the forces of hatred and violence in this world, and keep God's good faith to the last.

-- THE END --